www.trafford.com
North America & international
toll-free: 1 888 232 4444 (USA & Canada)
fax: 812 355 4082

Unique Episodes

in

My Life

My Autobiography

by Nancy Martin

My journey in life is unique.

It is my journey.

I dedicate this book to my Mother – who saved my life by taking care of me for seven years –

And to Betty Browning who encouraged my writing and proof read my book. She also gave my book its title.

Contents

Episode

A definition is:

Incident – a brief unit of action in a dramatic or literary work.

An event that is instinctive.

Syn. – an occurrence.

Prefix

I started this book at the suggestion of a few different people. They said your life has been interesting, write it down.

I am a Capricorn and should have never married a Gemini. I know that now. My second husband was an Aquarius. Neither handled money the way I would have. This creates discontent and anger on my part because I could have done better.

My first husband never came in the door and kissed me hello.

I would get phone calls and they would ask "Is Jerry there?" I would say "just a minute I'll check". Not knowing if he'd come in or not.

He said "I can't get close to the children." My answer was "when did you ever try?" You have to show kids affection if you want them to return it.

I decided if I can't trust my husband with money I probably can't trust him in other ways. I was right, he was playing around. One steady girlfriend throughout our marriage.

This is one thing I did wrong. I went to my high school dance and didn't know how to dance. (Take lessons before 18 years old.)

A few other mistakes I made were financial ones.

1) Gave up house. The value increased.

2) Didn't sue when daughter swallowed pin and needed surgery.

3) My Michigan fall on ice sent me to doctor too, didn't sue.

4) Supermarket injury, didn't sue.

5) Sold my T-bird too soon. Value went up.

This is something that happened in sister in law's family. A mother and father both died within six months of each other. No money or insurance. Their daughter and husband got stuck with both bills.

What have you accomplished in life if you can't even pay your own funeral bills or have insurance that will cover it? Why hurt your relatives?

My Mother decided to pay the funeral bill in advance for herself – rather than make large payments to an insurance company at her age of 80.

This story is in the family. People went to a funeral, and as the casket was being lowered a ventriloquist said, "Lower me down easy boys" and the pallbearers dropped the casket.

Husband Jerry called from Las Vegas once and said "I'm here." I said "thanks for telling me where you are." He hung up the phone in disbelief, and said to his friends "she wasn't mad at me." It was too late to stop him from going there I thought. He was already there.

After we split up I asked my husband "why he brought his girlfriend into our house?" He had no answer for that one. Later on I asked him if he ever asked her to marry him. He said, "No, I only suggested it, to string her along? Yes."

My first husband Jerry died in 1991 in Palm Springs, California of a heart attack two weeks after surgery. Too far gone, they couldn't fix his heart.

I should have thrown out my husband and saved my house myself years ago.

My first husband gambled way too much, Vegas, bookie and horses.

My second husband was a retired Navy 20 year man, Navy Seal and chief petty officer, and he drank too much.

Boy can I pick them. Better luck next time.

My book is interesting according to those that read parts

of it and said give me more to proof read to test it out.

My experiences are original and will entertain you.

Thank goodness I kept a goal in mind and didn't

give up.

I was born in Marion, Ohio, President Harding's hometown. Our family had three children. I was the middle one. We grew up there and I graduated from Harding High School. My Father was a newspaper pressman all of his life. I worked in a market for two years, moved to California to make more more money as a cashier for four years and worked. I then married, had two daughters, divorced after 13 years. Sold house! Moved too many times, and years later remarried. Heart attack killed first husband, second died of cancer.

I'm a stronger person for my rough life. But wouldn't want to go through it twice.

I've always felt that you should climb steadily towards your goals. It's taken a few years to gather information for this book. I have now met this goal.

Neither of my two husbands gave me a sense of security that I would have liked. – So I decided this book could give it to me – hopefully.

I've had many things happen in my life – some good, some bad. – If I could start over again I would definitely make some changes. All I can do now is put my life into a forward direction and think positive.

I'm writing this book while living in a nursing home, hoping to move out soon. I need my life to get better.

A smart cousin of mine said, "Most problems can be solved mathematically." Think about it a minute. He worked with the space program and fed information into the computers.

I read this someplace and jotted it down.

1) A good book informs you.

2) A superior book entertains you.

3) A great book changes your life.

You be the judge.

Was I successful?

1) Two families merge

   Coffee pot

   Family trauma

   Twins

   Fifteen minutes worry

   Three children

   Ear infections

   Broken finger

   California trip

   Florida trip

   Indian Lake

   State Fair

   Hatchet incident

   Roller Rink

   Indian Mounds

   Harding High School

   Freckle remover

   Two dates

   Marion Star Newspaper

My Mother was a "Taylor" and my Dad was a "Turner".

I asked my Mother once if there were any serious incidents that happened while she was growing up in a family of nine children. She said two children died before school age, not knowing why. Mother had one emergency. At age five she was swinging on the coffee pot cord. Her Mother saw the danger and pulled her away just as the coffee came down and scolded her arm. She paced the floor while waiting for the doctor, and kept repeating "I want to be sister Beryl or Ruby" or anyone else, because she hurt too much being herself.

Her sister Beryl got lost in a snowstorm on the way home from school. The neighbors had to all go out looking for her. They found her walking in a circle and ready to stop walking. The same child did two more things. She got her arm stuck in the wringer washer. It went up to her elbow. She also held onto the hay loft pulley and she went all the way up to the top. Tearing the ligaments on her fingers, she was in the barn. They had to fix her fingers into bent position permanently.

My Dad's brother lost an arm. He had broken it and the doctor wrapped it too tight and cut off circulation and had to amputate because of gangrene."

His other brother had two sets of twins a year apart. My Mother watched the first set while she went to hospital and had the second set. They had to be set apart in their swing sets. They fought like crazy if they got close. These two were boy and girl. Second set was two boys. He had four other children, two got polio and one of them died of bulbar polio.

My Dad's Mother also had two sets of twins – one set died, she got a bad case of poison ivy while pregnant and it killed the twins. If she hadn't been pregnant it would have killed her. Grandma had five children living.

17

They used to say years ago that twins skipped a
generation, they didn't in this case. No more Twins.

Grandma Taylor told her children when you get

married move across town. So I won't worry about you so

much. Don't move next door. She had nine children. She

also said "I worry about each family member for 15 minutes.

Then I turn them off and worry about the next one. She

also told her children to eat the crust of the bread because

it would make their hair curly. Most of her kids had curly

hair anyway.

Our family was a little bit different in getting childhood

diseases. We got the chicken pox three times, a few the

first time, more the second and lots of spots the third time.

Childhood

My Mother had three children. First my sister Marilyn, a nine month baby weight seven pounds. Then me two and half years later, a four pound two ounce seven month premature baby. I went hone weighing just three pounds 11 ounces. Mother caught a cold and coughing put her into labor. She headed for the hospital by cab and had me 30 minutes later. I was 16 inches long and fit in my sisters doll buggy. The doctor said no soap just baby oil for two months. She's ok just feed her. My aunt came in to help with the baby and said, she's too slippery and put me on a pillow to carry me. She was afraid she'd drop me. Premature babies don't cry, too weak. My Grandmother didn't think I would live, could only take two ounces of milk at a time, every two hours. The doctor said I would be behind the other kids my age until I was 10 years old.

My brother came along six years later and weighed in at

about nine pounds. He was a breach birth at eight months.
The doctors tried to turn him around but couldn't. The
effort put Mom into labor that day. The doctor said if the
baby wasn't born in five minutes it will be dead. He made
it.

My Mother said to the doctor, what do I do with her, she's
so little – me at three pounds 11 ounces.

Answer was no bassinette. Use a baby bed, drape blankets
over sides to keep out drafts. Rig two large juice cans with
small hole in one end insert a 20 watt light bulb into it,
other end open. Put one at foot and head of bed. Works
like an incubator.

Our neighborhood had several fruit trees and bushes.
Apple, cherry, grapes, plums and rhubarb, so my Mother
canned a lot. Also my Dad had a small garden by our
garage, with tomatoes and green onions in it.

My brother fell out of the apple tree once, didn't break

anything. Just knocked the wind out of him. He also had

many ear infections as a child and my Dad rigged a home

made heat lamp for him. He put a small light bulb in one end

of a large juice can after cutting a hole in it. And after

cutting the other end clear out, wrapped a magazine around

it and secured it with a rubber band, so no skin would touch

the metal can. He lost 10% of his hearing in one ear from so

many infections.

I remember watching electric storms from our bedroom.

One of our windows was high up and scary, when lightening

appeared. Thunder didn't help either. Sometimes we got to

play in the water along the curb with little boats if it was

warm enough after a storm in the daytime.

One day my sister and I were playing softball in front of

our house and the end of the ball hit my little finger and

21

broke it.

We had no fenced yard, so didn't have pets. Just two turtles named Pete and Repeat. Also a small fish tank with little guppies in it.

Here's a funny one I remember.

Dad liked to take a car ride to relax once in a while. He ran out of gas out in the country one night, near a farm house with a gas pump. It was late, so my Mother told him to stay with the car and get gas in the morning. My Mother thought it was a pretty stupid thing to do. So she took the children and hitched a ride home and left him with the car.

In 1946 our family made a trip to California. We delayed our trip for an extra week. I had just been exposed to the mumps. I took a boy's homework to him and he had the mumps. I arrived in California and got sick. I gave it to my uncle and his daughters. What a vacation! I spent mine in bed.

During the 1946 trip we saw a large tarantula spider in the desert and once had to stop during a sandstorm because we couldn't see.

We went to an uncle's farm near Mansfield, Ohio for a visit. We started to climb up in the hayloft and saw a huge snake. We made a fast exit out of the barn.

We also made a trip to Florida. Daytona Beach is very long.

Before heading home we went to Washington, D.C. and saw the Lincoln Memorial and the Washington Monument.

Mother told me I could never live in Florida. The mosquitoes ate me up. They have a tiny mosquito that comes through your screens, They're called no-see ums.

We went on a family vacation to Indian Lake, Ohio. I spent most of my time afternoon and evening at the roller skating rink. We took time out to rent a bicycle built for two for my brother Tom and me. It was fun.

My Mother liked the roller coaster and candy apples. She couldn't take any circular motion rides, they made her sick.

We went to the Ohio state fair in Columbus, Ohio once a year. One time we took home a small "green" lizard. You pinned him on your shirt. He changed color to "beige". We didn't know what to feed him. We found he liked live flies, hard to find in the winter time. I guess we should have gotten food from the pet store. We couldn't find him for a while, he was then found in our couch dead.

As teenagers we decided to take a bike ride one time – a long one. First mistake wearing shorts – we sunburned our upper leg. We arrived at our destination and one of us got a flat tire. We had to call one girls father to get him to pick us up in his truck. We didn't think to take a tire patch kit with us. We rode about five miles.

My Dad was cutting wood with a hatchet one day. He was standing too close to our backyard clothesline at the time. The hatchet bounced off the clothesline and came back and hit him in the head. The only time I ever heard him swear. Ouch!

The roller rink owner's son was under 15 state champion in Ohio for free style spinning and jumping. His little sister skated at our rink. She was four years old.

My Mother made me a beautiful skating outfit. Red corduroy jacket and skating skirt lined in white satin. While she was doing this, I made a long skirt in sewing class to match.

They had two rinks and three movies in Marion, Ohio. I liked the crystal rink, larger, but further from town and better for dance numbers. My Dad had to give me a ride to the rinks. Sometimes we got a ride home. The crystal rink was three miles out of town. – When I was there it was a town of 35,000. We also had a drive-in movie.

All my school years were spent living at 120 Carhart Street. I graduated from Harding High School in 1955. A new building was built to handle 1500 kids. I was the second graduating class from the new school. We had an Indian mounds burial grounds near the school. It had been dug up and it looked like a sugar bowl – we could ride our bikes down one side and up the other.

The President Harding Memorial is on the Boulevard in Marion, Ohio. His home is also there. We went through it in a group for a history class lesson.

I took a high school class to graduate – Spanish - one year – didn't think I'd ever use it – big mistake! I moved to California. Many Spanish there, should have taken second year to be able to speak the language.

Once in high school I bleached my hair blonde. Had to re-dye it. It turned green.

I learned to swim at the YMCA in Marion, Ohio. I was so scared of the water that I took the course twice to be pool safe.

I took drivers education in school. It was one semester. My Mother decided to learn at the same time and beat me. A friend next door taught her.

My Mother learned synchronized swimming to music and taught swimming too.

It was a complete surprise to me when my sister paid me the compliment of entering me in the "Miss Buckeye Lake" contest. Didn't expect to win, but it was fun. A bleached blonde won. I had the same blue bathing suit at home that she used to win.

My sister's boyfriend went into the service. He said to a friend, watch my girl while I'm gone! He did a good job. He married her!

My sister had a lot of freckles. My Mother gave her a surprise bottle of freckle remover on Christmas one year. It taught my sister to face life with a sense of humor.

As a teenager I goofed one day. I made two dates on one night. My Mother found out and grounded me for two weeks. She had to lie and say I was sick and couldn't go out to both guys. Upset with me – Yes!

My Mother pulled a good one one day. She ran the sewing machine needle right through her thumbnail, twice. She went to a neighbors house to get her to pull it out for her. She did. The first time through nail the needle had broken off.

My Dad worked on the Marion Star Newspaper as a pressman for years and is now retired and living in Marion, Ohio. He started out as a paper boy.

He always brought home two newspapers, one for him to

study and one for the family.

One of the men working with my Dad studied hand writing analysis. He got so good at it that some bosses were hiring and firing on his say so.

One newspaper employee fell with a candy cane in his mouth as a child and did permanent damage to his voice.

2) Market Jobs

First job Wises'

Tempted by California

Ralph's Market – toe injuries

Didn't feel safe

Fire

T. Bird

Ski trip

Ralph's happenings

Injury

Future husband

Divorce Mother

I worked in a large independent "Wises" Market for two years, after graduation, 48 hours per week. I lived at home and bought all my all clothes. Later on, my market burned down.

Encouraged by my uncle who was already working at Ralph's Market in California – He said I could make twice as much money working in California. I couldn't work in his store, he was manager! He found an opening for me in Downey, California and I stayed there for four years. Tired of walking the first year, I saved money through the second year and had $1,000 to put on my car which cost $3,000 – a 1957 Ford Thunderbird – white – removable hardtop. Loved it!

My Mother went with me on the bus to California, didn't want me to go alone. We stopped to see the Grand Canyon on the way.

31

While I was working in Downey I hit my little toe on the bottom of my ironing board and broke it. No car yet. I was still walking to work, every step hurt. The doctor taped two toes together.

I dislocated a different toe while swimming one day. I pulled it back into place. I saw the doctor the next day and he asked me who fixed it. I said "I did". I had a one bedroom apartment with a pool. I shared it with another girl. It was $100 per month. I still don't know what I did to dislocate my toe.

The next apartment we got was larger and fit three of us in extra large bedroom and was a little bit closer to work, and cheaper $120 divided by three.

I was twice followed while walking home in Downey. Once I heard footsteps turn around and start to follow me. Then I decided I needed a car.

I also found it was not safe to do laundry at a public
laundry in the evening with alleyway door open. I was
watched twice and made a fast exit out the front door.

While in small Downey apartment there was a fire that
put smoke into all apartments in one building. The gas
was paid and the manager turned on heat for all units in
her apartment. The cause was a man smoking on his
couch and fell asleep.

I went out to our wire clothesline and washed it before
hanging up my clothes one day. One other tenant said he'd
never seen that before. They do get dirty!

My 1957 white T bird drove great. I took it cross
country to visit family. The only thing that happened to my
car was the fuel pump went out. Had to put in a new one.
We took turns driving four hours each, my brother and I.
My car was a hardtop convertible with porthole windows
on the sides.

I tried skiing one time in my early twenties. My date thought it would be fun so we drove to the mountains. We went to Snow Valley. That's five miles after Running Springs, on the way to Big Bear Lake.

Knowing nothing about skiing, we rented skis. The rope tow pulled us up the lower practice hill. We let go of the rope and fell down immediately. You must place your right foot crossways on the hill before letting go of rope. On second try we did it. The next problem was stopping. I remembered from watching skiing on television. You point your toes together and push down against the snow like a snow plow. I made it down standing up. First lesson accomplished!

While working at Ralph's Market, I took some ballroom dancing lessons at the traffic circle in Long Beach, California. It was fun.

One customer lady switched margarine for butter and paid for margarine in carton. We discovered what happened when a lady paid for butter and got home with margarine, she reported the mistake.

One guy was handcuffed to my check stand one day for passing a bad check.

I also had to go to court and say I accepted a bad check – My initials were on the check. They paid my wages for the day.

One day we had a lady customer try to carry out a canned ham between her legs under her skirt. She was fat - but she dropped it.

Another one was funny. Someone ate a whole pumpkin pie and didn't get caught. Left the empty box on the counter.

After three years at Ralph's I became cashier of month. I went to LA to meet the boss. He gave me a gold mesh evening bag and had me add up a long list of numbers, timed me and said, "Smarty."

Another one was funny. I picked up a carton of milk and almost threw it over my head – It was half full and light weight.

While at work one day I received a bad blow to my head, on my forehead. Nothing broken. It kept me off work for a week. Then the doctor said put heat on it. I went in Uncle's pool, "at 90 degrees". The swelling went down the next day. Then I had two black eyes for another week. The guy that caused the injury got fired.

I saved $1,000 in a year's time and put it down on my car. It cost $3,000 and was two years old. New cost was about $5,000.

I met my future husband when he looked at my car and checked it out before I bought it. He was a salesman for Ford Motor Company.

I took the five hour trip to Las Vegas with him and got a speeding ticket doing 85 m.p.h. Cost me $40. I said "it's my first ticket" to the cop. He answered, "It'll be your last if you slow down."

My Mother left my Dad after 25 years of marriage. My brother came with her to California. I was already there.

Mother got a job at a drapery store and later worked at Sees' candy store.

My brother's favorite thing to do was gymnastics. My sister took piano lessons. Me I skated. (roller) My sister also sang in a trio group.

3) Medical problems

Snake bite

Tonsils

Eye surgery City of Hope

My husband, a gambler

Las Vegas marriage

I got a shot in the doctor's office one day and it really got red and hurt. The next time I told the doctor he should do it and not the nurse. Then I found out the nurse was his wife.

While in the Navy Jerry played golf near a hospital in Cuba. A rattlesnake bit him and they rushed him to the hospital. That and the fact that the snake had just eaten and venom was weaker saved him.

Just before I got married I had my tonsils out. I was working. So I set the surgery up for two months later and got some time off to do it. Every time I'd stop taking medicine I'd get sick again. Doctor said he knew I would have some trouble. But not this much!

While back in my room after surgery I suddenly threw up. The nurse sent my Mother to get help. Later the doctor said, no more adults tonsils!

39

My husband to be Jerry flew to the City of Hope in Chicago. He stayed two weeks. He had glaucoma due to previous injury. He had broken his nose playing football and the bone chips had moved up into the eye area and he blanked out and couldn't see. I had gone out with him only once before surgery. He wanted to get it over with before dating me again. The bone chips moved over a period of time – 15 years. They had to remove the chips.

The City of Hope paid for his surgery. He had to fly there. Jerry had a large family, about 12 children, only one sister.

When we got married we stayed in Las Vegas for several days. I had saved $20.00 to go home on. My husband took it and we turned around and went back to Vegas and stayed another two days.

At an earlier time before our marriage he sent home $1,500. He went home got it, went back to Vegas and lost it. That's a gambler! It's a five hour trip from Los Angeles.

We got married in the Little Chapel of the Flowers in Las Vegas, Nevada. My husband lost money and went broke right after marriage. Then won little back to pay hotel room so we could stay a couple of days. I got married in a white suit. I had all white accessories.

One trip to Vegas, we were still there and out of money, when my husband said, "Write a check for $200." I said "no the account is empty." He insisted and I wrote it. When we got home he then had to sell a car quick to cover the check and pay the rent. That's a gambler!

After marriage we moved into a small apartment near his work.

My gambling husband Jerry called once from Las Vegas – a five hour trip and said "I'm here." I said "thanks for telling me where you are." He was shocked, I didn't get mad. I figured he was already there. I couldn't change that fact.

4) First Apartment

   Beer can

   Tricycle

   Car stolen

   Brother Harold

   Salesman story

   No children?

In our first apartment building we had a friend and wife across from us. The wife cut her finger on the new beer can opener. She wrote to the company and complained. They sent her a case of beer and a guy to show her how to open them.

Here's another one – a little boy rode his tricycle into the pool. He was still on his tricycle when he hit the bottom. I don't remember who pulled him out.

My first baby was born December 1 – 1961 a daughter named Sandra 8 pounds – 4 ounces.

I had my first daughter. I quit my job and stayed home to watch my daughter.

One day I looked out to see our car and it was gone. I called my husband and he didn't have the car, he thought I had it and I said no. It was hot wired and stolen, a new Ford Company demo car. They found it in Hollywood three months later, stripped of everything. The personal things we lost was our baby troller and golf clubs. My husband was a car salesman.

We went to Las Vegas quite a few times. Then I said why
on't we do something different? He picked a Mexico trip.

Jerry's brother and wife came out for a visit. He walked in
he pool where it drops off and gets deeper and went under. We
idn't know he couldn't swim. Two girls pulled him out. He
vas embarrassed.

Jerry took brother Harold on a deep sea fishing trip on one
isit. They caught an albacore tuna.

My husband's work was one block away from our apartment.
~~He sold cars~~.

Here's a salesman's story. Always qualify your buyer!

A guy, "a sailor", his ship anchored off shore came into a
ar lot to buy a car. He said, "My shipmates authorized me to
uy 30 cars."

The stunned salesman thought he was kidding and ignored him.

44

So the sailor went across the street and bought 30 cars, from another car dealer.

The name of the game – check out your buyer – he may not look like he's got money. Check him out! First salesman lost a lot of money.

In our first apartment my first daughter was born. While pregnant my husband's friend told me that my husband didn't want children of his own. He just wanted to spoil other peoples children. What a thing to tell me! Very bad timing. He was spoiling her kids when he met me.

Eight pounds four ounces, my Sandi had a "hematoma" on her head when she was born. It was a large fluid blister. It scared me. But the doctor said it will absorb in about three weeks. It did, so was ok.

5) Mexico

   Mexico City

   Bullfight

   Race track

   Acapulco

   A Mexican Hawaii

   No heaters

   Pool moat

   Hi – divers

   Montezuma's revenge

My husband got together with two other couples. My

Mother watched Sandi. She was just one year old and we

went to Mexico for ten days, six of us. We were advised

not to drive. Bandits were robbing visitors. So we flew

to Mexico City and stayed at the Maria Isabella Hotel on

the 17th floor. You could look straight down – no balcony.

I had one year of Spanish in high school – didn't think I'd

ever use it! We had bottle water in the room.

We went to a bullfight and race track. To go out –

Mexico City dressed up more.

We flew to Acapulco and stayed at the Acapulco Hilton

on the beach. It was like a Mexican Hawaii. No heaters

in the cars. The bar was on the beach surrounded by a

swimming pool like a moat around it. It also had a

bridge to walk over on.

I bought two souvenirs, a white leather jacket and an aqua ring while in Mexico.

We sat having dinner and watched the Acapulco hi-divers (21) of them, dive into the water below, at high tide only so the water is deep enough to land safely. They usually only have one diver. This was an annual celebration. I forgot the name of the restaurant. We were there in December. It was warmer than Los Angeles.

My husband drank some bad water someplace and I called the desk and they sent up a thermometer. I took his temperature but couldn't read the foreign thing. (Take your own next time). He was sick so I called the desk and read it to them. They agreed and sent up medicine. He had to see an American doctor again after returning home.

I went to the beauty shop and the girl said here comes your uncle. I said no, husband. I asked her what she was putting on my hair. She said cervasa. I said, that's beer. It stiffens the hair when dry. That idea surprised me.

6) First House

House and robbery attempt

Baby doctor

Manzanita tree

Child happenings

Pet store mouse

Daddy's beer

Spaghetti fight

Baby aspirin

Convulsions

Tonsils and pin surgery

Green hair

White Cadillac

Robbery

Lightening

Halloween outfits

Homesteaded house

Pen-toss

Gemini husband

Over spending

Colorado vacation

We decided we needed a house so we started looking. We

chose a three bedroom two bath with pool. I didn't know it yet

but I was expecting my second daughter when we moved in. My

husband pushed me into the pool and I got upset! Mother said

pregnant. She was right.

One day in 1964 I looked out my front window and saw

three boys. Two of them got out of their car and headed down

the driveway. The driver took off! I met them at my back door

and said, "What do you want?" They were caught, so they

headed for the Stonewood Shopping Center three doors away.

It was a potential robbery in progress. Glad I was home that time.

My baby doctor had to race to the hospital with a police escort

to deliver a relative's baby. Guess what she said to the mother.

"I got dressed so fast I forgot my underwear."

Here's another funny one that happened to me. I called my

doctor and told her I'd just started pains every five minutes. The next thing she said was funny! She said wait! Don't come in until the nurses change shifts at 11 p.m. At this point I only had three hours to go.

When barely pregnant the first time I felt like a was going to pass out. I dropped to the floor to prevent injury. I sat there a few minutes, got up and was ok.

My Mother gave me a beautiful addition to my house, a manzanita tree. She made it herself. She found a manzanita branch in the woods. She drilled holes in all joints. Then she bought wisteria artificial flowers to insert in each hole. She bought a pot to put it in. It was black and gold. Then added a small bag of plaster and some smooth rocks. Also a bottle of glue to cement them in so my children wouldn't play with them. A very pretty gift. You start with three main branches on tree. She also poured bleach on branch to lighten it.

Sandra fell out of stroller as a small child.

As I was pushing her home with a new tricycle one day she got her toe caught in the front wheel spokes. I felt bad because I was pushing her.

Dawna fell out of shopping cart at the market one day. No bruises, she didn't break a blood vessel on her forehead. She scared me to death.

Dawna tripped at about age two and knocked a front tooth loose. She hit the metal floor stripping between carpet and kitchen flooring.

We met Billy Barty at the park one day. He was head of the little people.

I had an exterminator at my door one day checking for termites. He looked around and when he got to the garage door, he found them and said I almost lost my garage door. He drilled holes in the door and put some pasty stuff in the door to kill them.

My daughter brought a pet mouse home from the pet store one day. We put it in a cage in our garage. We didn't know it was pregnant. She had 13 babies and they all died. We didn't have anything in the cage for her to make a nest with. So they got too cold.

In the house I owned I put a nine foot planter between living room and dining area. It looked nice, let a nice breeze go through after cutting out the wall. Planter pieces were made in three foot pieces.

We put up what we thought was a safe iron fence around the pool area. Straight pieces from top to bottom and no cross pieces to climb on. My Dawna proceeded to test the fence. She put her head right between two pieces of the fence. I called the fence company and asked them to come back and measure the fence and put in more pieces if wider than five inches. He put in five new pieces at his expense.

One day a big desert turtle came walking down our gutter and

we didn't know anyone that had one. We had him in our backyard
for a year. He fell into the pool one day and got stuck in the skimmer
and we had to pull him out. He wandered out of our yard – Never
saw him again.

One day when my daughter Sandy was about four years old,
Daddy asked her to go get him a beer. She took it into her bedroom
and drank it. After waiting a little while Daddy yelled, "Where's
my beer?"

My Mother came for a visit one day. She sent me out of the
house on an errand. She then mixed some plaster of Paris up and
put my daughters hands in the plaster. When dry she spray
painted them gold. Nice gift.

While in my Chaney house I got mad at my husband once
and threw a plate of spaghetti at him across the room. He told
someone at work – "Well! She finally got mad at me!"

My girls got the chicken pox three times. First time, a few
spots. Second time a few more spots. Third time many spots.
think my brother did it too.

My dentist pulled a good one one day. He cut off several of
is fingers in his lawnmower. End of job.

My little daughter Sandi took 13 baby aspirin, orange flavored.
ll I had to do was count them. I had just bought them. Doctor
aid just give her lots of water. This was before child safety caps.
our baby aspirin equals one adult aspirin.

My two year old daughter Sandi was afraid of my sweeper
vhen she was little. I let her use if for a while, then she was ok.

She also said there was a face in my bedroom. The gold
ight stand knobs and handle did look like a face in the dark.

Uncle Harold had a cocker spaniel. It bit my Sandra. We
idn't know why – until later. She pulled his ears.

Baby Dawna was born in 1964. My daughter Dawna had

56

convulsions starting when she was about two years old. Every time her temperature went up over she went. The first one she was taking a nap in the bedroom, I heard a strange sound and ran to check her, picked her up and ran to the phone to talk to the doctor. I thought she was going to choke and put her face down across my lap. She began to come out of it. So I told the doctor and he said bring her in tomorrow. The danger is choking on the tongue. My husband was home the second time and put his finger in her mouth. They clamp down hard and are unconscious during a convulsion. After the second one I asked the doctor what the difference was between a convulsion and a seizure. He said, "the cause". An epileptic has damage to the brain and will have an attack when mentally upset. Dawna's convulsions were only with illness and temperature. The third time she was in back of our wagon and I'd just turned into my neighbors Mother's driveway. As I looked back I saw her fall over. I ran her in the house to the kitchen counter and got a spoon to hold her tongue down. She didn't look right as she came out of it so I put my finger in her mouth and pulled her tongue forward. The doctor told me to fix several tongue depressors, wrap with tape after padding with gauze or cotton and put in vital areas of house and one in purse. I did.

After the second one doctor did a brain scan. It didn't show anything.

This same daughter had medicine in every bottle from two weeks to three months. She had stomach cramps like colic. It stopped at three months. Doctor said it might.

Doctor said if she ever goes in and out of convulsions – bring her in fast if you can't handle it. She didn't have any more after we took out her tonsils.

My Sandi – age 6 – had bad tonsils so doctor decided to remove them. I said what about Dawna's? He said yes, let's prevent what we can with that child. He gave them vitamin K to help clot blood a few days prior to surgery. He didn't keep them overnight. In at

seven a.m. out by five p.m. As I was about to take them home he

a said they could hemorrhage.*^{n}* I said thank you. I put one on couch,

other on love seat and watched them all night. They did ok.

While I was shopping one day at Penny's, my daughter Dawna

said, "Sandi swallowed a pin." I said, "What?" Sandi said, "what's

the matter with that?" I said, "for one thing it's sharp!"

The doctor found the pin with second x-ray try. He waited

ten days hoping it would come out. It didn't. She was still six

years and sister was four years old. They operated to remove it.

I said what about appendix. He said it was large, so removed it.

My question – What if Dawna didn't tell me?

My daughter Sandi had platinum blonde hair. It turned green

from pool chemicals in water. I decided to rinse her hair with

diluted bottled lemon juice. It took out the green. I made a strong

solution at first, stuck ends of hair in the bowl, waited a few minutes

then diluted it and poured over all of her hair.

When school started I had no car. A friend loaned me her white Cadillac. I took my daughter in and went back to the car, turned it around and started to drive home. A lady by the curb said, "Whose car do you have?" I stopped and looked and saw another car just like mine. We traded cars. My "key" worked in her car! That's a scary thought. What if I had driven it home?

My baby sitter had a scare one night while I was gone. The lights went out. She grabbed the kids and ran into the bathroom and locked the door. After it did it to me twice the electric company put a new transformer on the light pole.

This same friend Helen was robbed one night. They got in through her bathroom window. They turned on lights as they went through her house. A neighbor got suspicious and called her house and got no answer. It scared them and they left in a hurry. Her television fell off the back of the truck. They took a jug of change, some silverware and a fur coat that was insured. So they didn't cost her too much. But she got scared and sold her house and moved to South

Downey.

Another incident happened at her new house. Lightening struck

a block away. It cracked her picture window and knocked her

chandelier onto her table and damaged it. We found out where it

struck and went to see the damage a block away. A lady was

sitting at her window sewing. The lightening came down a palm

tree and split it in half. It dug a ditch in the ground over to an

apartment building and blew the hinges off all the doors, it was a

new building. The lady got her nose cut pretty badly when the

glass window broke.

I also heard of a lightening strike that hit a swimming pool. A

person in center of the pool didn't die.

I made Halloween outfits for my daughters on year. My Mother

sent me a cute card and I copied it. I had a jack-o-lantern and a black

cat. Both outfits started out with long sleeve shirts in black and long

black pants and black shoes. The cat needed a black hat with ears, nittens and tail, and I painted black whiskers on her face. The

ack-o-lantern needed an orange body. I put elastic in top and bottom

em and stuffed it with newspapers. I got another idea later to stuff

t with small balloons. For the face I sewed on a black mouth and

ad also a white piece so I could cut out the teeth. I used a zig-zag

titch on face. I made a cut out piece with a green stem for hat and

sed color orange on her cheeks. My ~~Sandi~~ *Dawna* wore the jack-o-lantern

o Halloween party at school and won first place in originality in

econd grade.

The next year my Mother came by and asked to borrow my

ack-o-lantern outfit and said she was going to a party. She enlarged

he body part with more orange material so it would fit Grandpa and

nade a large stem to fit over his head with edging orange on bottom

f stem so it looked cut out. He sat down in a chair and they thought

e was part of the Halloween decorations. My Mother made up as a

lack cat and found a full face mask to go with it.

The next year I made a witches dress and bought a hat. Then put white shoe polish on Sandi's face. The little one I made into a ghost, that was easy.

While we were living in Downey, California my husband started to open up a restaurant with his brother Harold. There was a fire the night before we took it over, cigarette in waste basket they thought. The first owner got the insurance money and left – we had nothing – So we had to close down. He'd planned to have his brother run it and he could bring in customers from his car business. His brother Harold died before it could happen.

Jerry had a lawyer "homestead" our house so the creditors couldn't touch it. They can't take the one house you're living in!

One day my Sandi threw a pen across the room to her sister and it hit her right in the corner of her eye, scary! The next day she said my eye isn't right. I took her to the doctor and he gave me some medicine. Then told me it was a good thing I came in with her.

My daughter Dawna cut her head on the shower door frame. Needed a couple of stitches. Later found out her big sister pushed her.

I gave Jerry a paper on the Gemini horoscope one day for his birthday one year. He read it and said, "Now that you've got me figured out – I'm not changing!"

He loaned my Union Oil credit card to a friend to take a trip one time. Then we couldn't pay the bill and I lost my card.

He overdid the charges on his American Express credit card one time and I took it and cut it up into many pieces with my scissors in front of him!

Family security first please!

We went to Grandma's house in Estes Park, Colorado one Christmas. We had our tickets bought and my daughter Sandi got sick. We went anyway. Took her to the doctor when we got there. Grandpa took us out in the woods to get our Christmas tree. The rangers mark which trees can be cut down. Then they sell tickets for $2.00 and let the people thin out the forest. We took our tree home and my daughter Dawna watched Grandpa cut a few branches off the bottom of the tree so he could put them

where they were needed. She watched him for a while then she

said, "It's the first time we ever had to make a tree."

My Sandi found a great way to spend the afternoon. They

made an artificial slide at the YMCA. They turned on the hose,

propped it up in the air and let the water freeze. It made a large

slide to go down on and a long way to walk back to climb up the

ladder and do it again.

Mother took the children for a horseback ride one day. On the

way back the ranch owner said, hold your horses. We were within

sight of the barn and the horses knew it. They started to run.

Sandi's was first. Then Dawna's horse turned sideways and Dawna

slid off and hit the ground. She didn't get hurt, thank heavens.

~~I got a comment from neighbor, watch out for Betty, husband's girlfriend. I then knew. Darn him.~~

65

7) Plane Trips

   Older plane engine fire

   Snow storm

   Coffee spill

   Grandmother

   A new co-pilot

I had several things happen on plane trips. One trip they shut down one engine coming in over Las Vegas. Fire was shooting out of it. I could see it.

One time coming into Denver the pilot said, "It is snowing in Denver." We're landing in a storm. The pilot circled a few times before landing. We made it ok.

There were a few accidents on the main road – car rollovers. We made it up to Estes Park, seventy miles from Denver.

One time the plane hit an air pocket and spilled coffee all over the kitchen. No coffee for lunch. We were over the continental divide coming to Denver that time.

My Grandmother always said she would never fly. Her daughter Beryl went to see her one day and said we have a ticket for you. Would you like to fly to Colorado for Christmas? She thought about it for a minute and said, "Yes, I think I'll go." They were in shock. They had to run and get another ticket quick. They wanted to ask her first. My Mother was very surprised when she picked them up at the airport. Guess where Grandma spent her trip, up in the cockpit with the pilots. She decided flying wasn't so bad after all!

8) Earthquakes

A 6.5 hit

The ground moved

Big Bear 4.5

Shower surprise

I was living in another house in North Downey when a quake woke us up at 6 a.m. It was about 6.5 on the Richter scale. A six is so much in strength, a seven is double the power. I had a crack above every doorway in the house and my linen cupboard doors were swinging back and forth. My kids thought Daddy was shaking the bed to wake them up for school. The paint store window was broken and the grocery store, across the street. Many things fell off the shelves. They served a cold lunch to the children at school – didn't turn the gas on that day.

During the same quake and airplane was coming in to land at Los Angeles airport and the pilot saw the ground move. Denver was instantly called and my stepfather a traffic controller called my Mother. She in turn called her sister in L. A. area. The jolt knocked a picture off the wall and threw her out of bed. She was standing in the doorway ready to run when the after shock hit. It wasn't safe to dive under her dining room table because her china cabinet tipped over and all the broken glass was under the table. After the first quake they turned off the gas in the whole apartment building. We were quite a ways away and didn't feel the after shock, an hour after the first quake hit.

My aunt was standing in her doorway ready to run when the after shock hit. She was nearer to the center of the quake. She learned the hard way, should have bolted the china cabinet to the wall. Tall bookcase cabinets likewise.

After I left Big Bear they had an earthquake with the strength of a 4.5 on the scale. That doesn't sound too bad but it shook all the fireplaces loose in Big Bear and everyone was warned not to use their fireplaces until they were checked out for safety.

I wondered if someone in the family would be someplace crazy when a quake hit. It happened! One member was in the shower one time and ran out in the backyard naked! They tell you to get away from glass. She had a glass shower door.

71

9) Entertainment

Tijuana

Disneyland

Knott's Berry Farm

Wax Museum

Hearst Castle

Catalina Island

Los Angeles Zoo

Marineland

Capistrano Mission

Universal Studios

Hollywood etc.

Coconut Grove

Chi-Chi Club

Paladium Ballroom

Las Vegas

Palm Springs tour

Rose Parade

We went shopping in Tijuana, Mexico. San Diego is five miles from the border. All the little shops are fighting for business. You can Jew the prices down and find good bargains. Leather jackets, purses and rings are good deals.

We saw Disneyland and Knott's Berry Farm many times. Disneyland is in Anaheim. Knott's is in Buena Park nearby. Knott's has a nice steak house and a good chicken dinner restaurant with boysenberry pie and jelly. Buildings are like a ghost town. I've been on the mine ride. Its newer than some of the original things.

The Wax Museum is also in Buena Park. Its life size wax figures, Frankenstein, Alan Ladd, Dr. Zhivago's Ice House scene, etc. etc.

There's another place that has fancy old cars in it like the Batmobile and old movie stars cars etc. I haven't seen this place. I think it's in Buena Park too.

We went to Hearst Castle with another couple. It's quite a place, one swimming pool was outside with marble statues. The other one was ten foot deep inside with tile decking and tennis court on top. He also had his own zoo. They said it would take three tours to go through it all. We took one. It was below San Francisco so we'd had a very long ride already from Los Angeles. There were no air conditioners in buildings in those days.

I think they have turned the castle over to the state and are letting them run it now.

I think they kept one cottage for the family to use.

The castle is 100 miles below San Francisco, near the ocean.

We took nephew David and Dad Harold to Catalina and David suddenly spotted the boy from the Lassie show and then he got mobbed for autographs.

We went to Catalina Island another time with Debbie my niece. We rode horseback around the bay and it started to rain. I took off my wig and my wool sweater, as soon as we came in. We were going to ride the new air boat home, but it broke down and we had to wait 'til smaller boat could take us, about 10 or 11 o'clock. The pavilion had Teresa Brewer singing in it, we didn't see her.

The Wrigley home is on the island. All homes have Spanish roofs.

Its two hours to go 26 miles on the big boat ride going over to Catalina, a faster return. From shore it's hard to see the island. I think you can fly from the center of island. I think I saw water planes near the boats as we docked. We also saw some glass bottom boats that we could ride in.

Some children were diving for pennies beside the big boat coming in.

We went to the Los Angeles Zoo. They had a train ride there.

In Marineland we saw dolphins plus seals etc. etc. – doing tricks. We saw whales, black and white, in San Diego.

We saw the Capistrano Mission where the swallows come back every year at the same time. It's a mystery how they do it.

We went to the Brown Derby Restaurant in Hollywood and saw eve Allen and another time saw Mugsy from black and white ovies. There are pictures of stars on walls.

We also went to restaurant row, a nick name for a street in ollywood that's all restaurants. We ate at the Captain's Restaurant, m Gilligan's Island. He was there.

We also took the tour of the Universal Studios one time, it's interesting.

We went to dinner at the Aku-Aku Restaurant, also on restaurant w, island, oriental food.

Another place we saw is Graumans Chinese Theater, stars' footprints front and stars' names on sidewalks, its in Hollywood.

The Coconut Grove was a special place to go for entertainment. We w singer, Johnny Mathis, blind piano player – Ray Charles, singer lla Reese and Jerry Lewis, not performing but so close to me I uld have touched him.

We also went to the Chi-Chi Club in Palm Springs and saw Jane Russell in a red sequin dress with detachable skirt.

While still working, I went to the Paladium in Hollywood with my Uncle Sydney and wife and I got to dance with one of Lawrence Welk's band members.

We also took tour of Hollywood homes.

We went many time to Las Vegas and stayed at the Tropicana Hotel. One of the first hotels you see driving in from Los Angeles. It's a five hour ride to get there from L. A.

We also took the tour of Palm Springs homes one day. Liberace, Elvis, Sinatra etc. etc. Gene Autry has a hotel there. Bob Hope's home is one of the largest. He's up on a hill by himself. Sinatra lived on Frank Sinatra Drive.

We went to the San Diego Zoo to see Shamu the whale.

We also went to Marineland of the Pacific to see smaller water animals.

77

We took the children and went to see the Rose Parade in Pasadena one year. My husband had a friend that lived two blocks from the main parade route. We were standing right where the floats and bands come together just before they go on camera for television. The floats on one road and the bands on another. My girls were in grade school then. Many people were sleeping in sleeping bags all night on the front lawns of houses along the parade route. This friend invited us to dinner. It was a fun day.

10) South Downey House

300 – 500 club

Problem solving – Debbie

Problem solving friend

South Downey – police

Porch puppy – job

Watts riot

Poodle puppies

Girlfriend – Gemini horoscope

Girlfriend

My husband was a good car salesman but he gambled too much! Race track, Las Vegas and bookies, he did them all. Not good for the budget at all.

He came from a large family of 12 – one older sister and the rest boys. We went back to see his Mother when Sandi was about one and half years old. She died three months later. His Father died when he was eight years old.

One day I said to my husband, "If you're so good, where's my car?" and he got me one. Some of his buddies had been telling me how good he was. He sold enough cars to be in the Ford 300 – 500 Sales Club. They rented the Palladium Ballroom in Hollywood for a special night out. Dinner and gifts. That meant he'd sold over 300 cars in one year. 365 would be one a day.

My niece Debbie made a good decision when she took a psychology class in college to add it to her teaching credentials. She wanted to know how to solve problems and decided how to teach in the first to sixth grades.

She solved one problem this way. A boy kept walking down the hall and banging on her door and running. Noting when it occurred she opened the door and grabbed him. Told him he would stay in this younger classroom for the day and do everything they did all day! He never did it again! A smart solution.

Also another solution was Debbie's Dad might need his hearing checked. So his children started whispering around the house, so he went to a doctor.

This solution to a problem worked. A friend had his nephew come to his house. He came out of bedroom with his pants hanging low and the friend said "not in my house". He pulled his pants to the floor. The kid went back to his room. He came out again looking the same way. The friend said "I said no!" and pulled his pants to the floor again. He didn't do it again. They say make the punishment fit the crime committed.

My niece Debbie figured out that my daughter Sandi was a leader, not a follower. Why didn't the school figure it out? I also read that a Sagitarius is a bad influence on the next child.

Excuse me – there was another house between mine and the apartment in Bellflower.

A South Downey house I rented for $250 including yard work.

I got a policeman at my door, asking me if I had a blonde daughter. I said "should I admit it?" He said "don't panic!" Then he told me what happened. Five children had put a bunch of junk in some neighbor man's swimming pool. It was very dirty, they didn't think he cared much! The bad one was a bag of cement! My question was why was the pool open to children? Very dangerous! That's probably what the police said to the owner. No charges were pressed. First offense. She went to police station.

My daughter brought home a puppy one day. She picked up the puppy out of a cage where they leave unwanted animals at the

the pound. She put it on my front porch and said "Look what somebody left us."

I didn't know she knew how to get to the pound on her bike!

I tried to go back to work once and guess what happened. The manager asked if I had any experience. I said "yes, if you don't mind it 15 years ago." He hired me but I didn't know he had a girl off sick. He let me go two weeks later. I was crushed!

During the Watts riots my family went to the Pike Amusement Park in Long Beach. After wandering around for a while they asked everyone to leave, to stop trouble before it happened.

I drove to the airport one day and had rocks thrown at my car. My husband took his brother and wife to the airport another time and they threw rocks at their car. One came in the car and glanced off the back of my husband's neck. We decided to hereafter take the freeway. It was too dangerous.

My husband brought me a little poodle. White and only weighed five pounds. She cost $50 with an agreement that the owner gets

one poodle, of her choice, from the first litter. She took a female.

Mating with one of her dogs, my dog had five puppies, one died,

the first one. I called a vet and said its taking too long. I see a

foot. He said grab the foot and pull. I was afraid it would break

it was so little. She delivered four healthy puppies. We kept the

male runt of the litter. He weighed about three ounces.

They weighed about three and half ounces about the size of

a baby kitten. I weighed them on my postal scale. Mother

weighed five pounds on regular scale.

neighbor said watchout for Betty !

My husband really pulled a good one. He had this girlfriend

through all of our marriage. She had a husband and two children.

They came over to our house as a family and I didn't tumble at

first. I assumed he was faithful. I was the only girl he married.

When we were about ready to split up I found an article in

the Journal Magazine on the Gemini horoscope. Everything fit

84

him. He was shocked as he read it. His following statement was, "Now that you've figured me out I won't change"! He didn't marry this longtime girlfriend. But did get another girl with her same horoscope, another Gemini – like the first one.

This girlfriend of his tried to push me. She said on the phone one day, "We know what we're doing. When I say jump he jumps. I have control!" I thought to myself, maybe its time to find out. The next time he came back I told him exactly what she said. Knowing he wouldn't like it. They got in a big fight. He came back and said "you're pretty smart!"

I asked my husband later on – "Did you ever ask her to marry you?" He said, "No! I only suggested it."

The girlfriend and I changed places. I became the other woman. His buddy said he wants what he doesn't have. A challenge!

One warning to wives. If your husband suddenly dresses up for girlfriend watch out. Mine did it.

11) Bellflower Apartment

Horseback ride

Accidental mating

911

Halloween house

Daughter's art talent

One day my daughter Sandi went horseback riding and came home with a broken arm. The doctor called it a green stick fracture, splintered but still in place, so no cast, he just put a sling on it. It was broken above the elbow. As my daughter put it after thinking it over – "It could have been my neck Mom." To which I said "yes". Her horse didn't like gates or fences and threw her off.

While in this apartment Sandi ran from a dog that was chasing her and hit her toe on the corner of the building and broke it.

When we went to the pet store one day we saw and heard a black mina bird. He had learned to swear and talked to everyone that entered the store.

In Bellflower apartment my poodle mated accidentally with another person's dog and had puppies that were too large for her. She had a Caesarian delivery, medication stopped her. We had milk. to bottle feed three and half ounce puppies the size of baby kittens, tiny glass bottles, rubble nipples.

I had a lady neighbor come to my door and ask for 911. She was very pregnant. She just started pains every five minutes. A fire truck rescue came and took her to the hospital.

In another apartment I met a lady that had her tailbone broken during childbirth. I never heard that one before. The baby got a scar on the top of her head from the pressure.

While in Bellflower I went to the laundry. While there I saw a man staring at me from the back alley doorway. I picked up my things and made a fast exit out the front door. Take a lesson from me. If washing clothes at night, park in front parking lot only.

In same apartment Halloween was fun. I put a sign on the door that said "Haunted House" with a ghost wrapped around it. I put on a "Halloween music record". Then I placed my ironing caddy near the door and put a witches dress and hat on it, plus an ugly witches face mask. The first child that came to my door screamed and ran back down the steps. Have a low light in the room for this effect.

Sandy's junior high school art teacher told his class to draw a hand. My daughter did so well she surprised him. She had every wrinkle done on it.

She also did a picture of a horse and had every muscle labeled and it looked perfect.

The teacher asked me if Sandy had any art training. I said no.

My other daughter Dawna won a poster contest, drawing a roadrunner.

My husband and I were separated at this time. He came over to see us one day and his girlfriend caught him and put a note on his car, "Should've gone to work."

12) Big Bear Lake

   B. B. snow

   Break in

   No frig

   Snow plow – driveway

   Joey's house

   Jerry's injury

   Spelling bee

   Sandi – float

My first initiation into Big Bear living was to be buried in snow at Thanksgiving time. My husband drove back down the mountain to go to work and it took him five hours to get there, should have taken him two hours.

I stayed in a lodge opposite Big Bear Hotel. They put me into large building. They could rent the smaller units easier. Ooops! It was a red ant hill.

on

I went down the mountain one day and returned up the mountain that night. I put my lights down at every passing car. Except one! And it was a cop. He turned around and caught me. Another car goofed and he caught him too.

My second initiation into Big Bear living was to have an attempted break-in where I was staying. Two dogs – Irish setters – and my porch light and my telephone saved us.

1) I heard dogs barking in yard behind me. I looked out front window and saw a guy standing near my telephone wires. I

91

ran to the phone and called police and told them where I was, quickly! They drove through and didn't see anyone the first time and they left.

2) I heard the dogs again and called again. On the second trip he saw him and put him in his gun sights, but let him go, then he looked around and saw my front screen was broken.

3) The third time the policemen were ready. The second policeman dropped off my policeman and sent him to me – he went back to the station, no car to be seen. The policeman said "Can I come in?" I said "Be my guest!" He left my door open a little, ready to run through. He dialed the police number ready to call for help, only one number left to call. We waited and watched window area. All of a sudden we heard a noise. Out went the cop and he grabbed the boy – what a relief!

4) The policeman told me another cop was on his way up the mountain to help if needed that night.

5) He also told me the boy had Charles Manson pictures on his

bedroom walls and he was about 18 years old.

6) This was not my favorite thing to be doing at 2 a.m. – Scary!

The telephone wire box cover was on the ground the next

morning when we looked. That scared me.

The first house I moved into had no refrigerator so I put my

perishables in a pile of snow. It worked for a week or two.

My ex came by and gave me his $500 bonus check one day.

I picked up some furniture at the second hand store with

the money.

His girlfriend found out and was very mad about it. *The check*

I went out on a date once. He came flying up the mountain

to see which employee I was with. It was the boss, surprise!

One day I plowed out my driveway and went out to do my

laundry. I came back and found the snow plow ready to bury

me back in again. I got out of car and waved at him to keep going

and bypass me. He did! Thank heavens once was enough. I

didn't want to shovel snow twice.

At the bowling ally dance area I danced with a guy who had been working on the fire line in a L. A. fire. He was a good dancer and I said "Where did you learn to dance like that?" To which he answered, "We do have other things in Wyoming besides wide open spaces."

While in Big Bear it was pretty cold during the winter. We decided to make Joey, my dog, a house. We found a box about his size. We cut open a doorway. We didn't have to coax him into it. After putting a pillow in it, he walked right into it. Like he owned it! At a later date he decided it was too cold. So he pushed the pillow up to block half of his doorway, clever little guy. A lot of fun! Joey was a Pekinese poodle mix and weighed about eight pounds.

Jerry my first husband came out of a Palm Springs restaurant one day and was jumped by two Mexicans. One hit him over the head with a crow bar. He grabbed the guy that hit him and pulled him into the restaurant. He called for help himself. He was bleeding but no one helped. By tapping the first guy's phone the police caught the second guy. The doctor said the first blow should have killed him. The lump on his head was about an inch high.

My daughter Dawna entered a spelling bee in junior high school. The prize for the winner was a trip to Disneyland. My daughter was ready to win but she deliberately misspelled the last word so the other girl could get the trip.

She was also in the top group in going for the Miss Big Bear title. She helped another girl make it and didn't push herself.

Sandi was on a Big Bear Lake parade float. Fourth of July parade I think.

13) Moonridge – Big Bear

Spiders and bat

Dawna Vitamin C

Shovel

Fire – friend

Vet

Flat tire

Nine mile fire

Beau-Beau

A Capricorn characteristic

Big snow one and half foot

Dyed poodles

Local animals

Real cat – dead mouse

Black poodle

Accident B. B. L.

Hot iron

Motor mount

Hepatitis

Gas station

Black ice

Flatlanders

Tree fell

Celebrity ski

Fourth of July parade

No brakes

Sandi accident

Raccoon excuse

Four wheel drive

Boulders

Hot coffee

Hair dye

Dog ears

Dawna contest

I moved into a house in Moonridge ski area. My daughter was dressing one morning, she let out a scream and threw her shirt. Upon checking we found a daddy long legs spider inside her shirt.

My landlord stopped by one day and said one of his tenants told him he was leaving to find a house with no spiders. He said good luck!

I had a bat in my house in Moonridge, he came in the upper story window and then came downstairs. My two girls screamed, ran into the bathroom and shut the door. This made me deal with the bat. I grabbed a jacket and threw it over my head. Then I opened the front door so he could get out and he left! He was flying so fast you could hardly tell where he was.

I kept a bottle of vitamin C tablets in my kitchen cupboard. My daughter Dawna decided to try it one day. She later told me she didn't catch a cold all winter. Her girlfriend got sick.

Here is one for everybody. Don't lay down your shovel in your yard and then get snow. We walked the whole yard and couldn't find it one time.

I got a call one morning from a friend that just survived a bad fire. They were all in the living room trying to heat and cook on a small propane stove. It sparked as they lit it. She grabbed two children and ran next door to call fire department, left them and ran back for two more, told husband to forget the fire and he grabbed fifth child and ran outside.

The firemen arrived in five minutes and told her it was a good thing she got out quick. The suction reaction of the fire might have prevented her from opening the front door later. The fire went to living room drapes and up the stairs. Had the children been in their beds upstairs they would have had to go out the windows. All were in the living room.

At an earlier time in Downey, California I was told by a fireman – a good thing to know. Indoor outdoor carpeting, the green stuff is very very flammable. In the situation I knew of it was put on a floor of a Lanai porch area.

I took my two dogs to the vets one day and walked back to the car, put them in the rear door of wagon and slammed the door quickly so they wouldn't jump out. I smashed my finger in the door, ouch! I went back into the office to make another appointment. The girl said you better sit down. I said "why, did I blank out?" She said yes. I didn't expect such a reaction with only a smashed finger.

I had a flat tire in Big Bear one day and thought back to the day before when I had just driven up the mountain, scary! A flat tire could throw you off the mountain.

I checked my tires better after that and always checked all liquids.

I had a friend that almost wrecked her car on the mountain. As she started off the road her arm got stuck in the steering wheel and woke her up.

We had a fire that got to within nine miles of Big Bear. We saw a red glow over the hill. I didn't know it but my Sandi put all her money in her pocket in case she had to leave.

My little poodle "Beau Beau" got hit by a car in front of our house in Moonridge. He weighed about four pounds. So cute. A sad day.

I know one lady in Big Bear that is a lot like me. She's a Capricorn. One day she said "I get so involved." I said I know what you mean. Example: She made napkins for a picnic, then made a tablecloth to match, then she looked at me and said I want your shirt, to me. It was red checked too. She tried to trade me for it.

While in Moonridge house we had a baby squirrel fall out of one of our trees. We put him in a box with food and water but he only lived three days.

We woke one morning to one and half foot of snow on the ground and still snowing.

A friend spent the night on the couch. He looked at his truck and decided it wasn't going anywhere. He was snowed in! He was supposed to be plowing snow. The shutters blew open, and his waterbed froze at his house in three days time.

I walked to small market with a box tied to a sled, about three small blocks away. It took five days to clear the road!

My landlord said with this size storm, clear the gas meter! It had icicles all around it from roof.

My Dawna got stuck in a snow bank at my Moonridge house. She was screaming but we were inside and didn't hear her. We went outside and had to pull her out. Luckily she had on her ski pants so didn't get too cold.

My daughter Sandi did a funny one one day. I came home to find my poodles had been rinsed with food coloring and were ready for Christmas – red and green.

We had a large dog that usually stayed outside and a cat. The cat jumped to my couch and then to the top of my china cabinet to get away from the dog one day.

I brought home groceries and set my purse down to open the door and I put food down and started to get more and looked at my purse and found I had a chipmunk in it.

One day there was a raccoon in my shed and we fed him a donut and he left, after dumping over my charcoal bucket. They're mischievous devils! – in constant motion.

While in Moonridge our cat jumped on a boyfriend's back. I guess he was protecting my daughter.

One day I saw a dead mouse under my dining room table. I mentioned it to someone and they said your cat brought you a present. That kind of gifts I can do without!

Near Safeway downtown I suddenly looked to the open area behind the houses and saw a "large" beige real cat. He was big! I didn't go any closer.

One day we drove from Big Bear down to Apple Valley pound. We were looking for another guy's dog that was missing. I said

"I hope they don't have a little black poodle." They did! I took him home for $15.00. He weighed four pounds. Full grown he weighed eight pounds. He was perfect. He was mixed breed and his hair wasn't as curly as a regular poodle, easier to comb. I came in the house one day and my daughter said "look Mom!" The dog was standing by the washer and a bottle of whisk had tipped over and poured soap all over his head. I said "into the bathtub quick!" I was worried about his eyes. That's strong soap.

He wandered away one day and we never saw him again. A sad day for me. I hope someone took him and took care of him.

I had another strange happening while in Moonridge. I came home to find that my iron had overheated. One of my girls must have left it on. The aluminum melted onto the ironing board and was a big ball of metal. The ironing board was metal, so didn't start a fire. Scary. This iron's electric cord had been taped. Maybe that's why it melted.

I got involved in one other person accident. I looked both ways then checked again. No one was moving in the whole block. I pulled out to turn left and suddenly hit another car. It was driving in the wrong lane on the wrong side of the road. How did he get there? Where did he come from? I had a friend standing near by answer my question, "Who was there first" he said "You were." That means he saw me and reacted wrong. The boy told the girl driving to go around me. That put them in the wrong lane. "Where did he come from?" was answered by my friend. They pulled out from behind a parked van. We both entered traffic. I was there first, he should have stopped. Instead he put himself right in front of me. My car cost $300 to fix.

We exchanged names and phone numbers. I explained to DMV - He jumped in front of me and was driving on the wrong side of the road, and they left me alone. It was his fault.

I drove down the mountain one day, something was wrong with the car. It was shaking. I took it to a gas station mechanic and asked him to drive it around the block and tell me what was wrong. He did and said your motor mount is loose. That's all I needed, to have the engine fall out of the car on a mountain road.

My older daughter got hepatitis. Don't know how. The doctor said the liver is in trouble. Eat no spices or grease for a few weeks. Let the liver recover! A big help.

As prevention the public health nurse in Big Bear Lake gave my other daughter and I gamma globulin shots.

My sister's daughter got hepatitis one time and her doctor didn't tell her to do anything. Her doctor didn't know.

While in Moonridge house I went to the gas station one day to see what my bill was and the wife said which one? Another woman was charging gas to my husband's name. I knew who it was.

Driving in downtown Big Bear Lake one night I saw a car sliding slightly and spun completely sideways! I wanted to slow down before getting to where he was. I didn't know I was also on black ice.

The first time I saw a ski rack on top of a car behind me I thought it was a policeman.

One of the local guys at the gas station yelled at me as I left. "Watch out for the flatlanders"! My mind went what? Oh! The ones that live off the mountain.

I hit the main road again near McDonalds, going the opposite direction and on ice, a car pulled out to make a left turn and stopped right in front of me. I had no brakes on ice so I aimed at his rear bumper. He waited a few seconds then made his left turn. Thank heavens! I just missed him. He must have been a flatlander. Locals would know better than to do something like that with icy roads.

A tree fell down one night. About a block down the road. It split a house in half at about 2 a.m. Everyone ran out to look.

The school bus almost slid into the lake one morning. So they decided to cancel school quicker next time.

My youngest daughter learned to ski while in Big Bear. The ski teacher was furnished. I had to rent her skis for each lesson.

The annual celebrity ski is fun. The movie stars come in to ski with other famous people and locals. My daughter almost ran into the son from the Eight is Enough show. She didn't know who he was until he took off his mask in the snack bar.

Another star rode up the ski lift and yelled at my daughter Dawna. "How do you do this?"

This happened on the fourth of July parade day. Everyone was having fun riding horses. They didn't think anyone would bother them. A policeman came up to my daughter Sandi and said "Drunk driving on a horse?" He then proceeded to write up a ticket, she was drinking a beer, under age of course. I had to go down the mountain with her and see somebody before paying the ticket. He looked at me and said "Some of the girls are worse than the boys." I said "I know." Paid him and left.

This was a scary day! I came down a hill from Moonridge. And I suddenly had no brakes. I looked on both sides of the road for a place to stop my car. I didn't want to hit the main road ahead of me. Too much traffic! I lucked out and found a chain link fence at a small apartment building and pulled into it. The main highway was next. I stretched 37 feet of fence. It didn't break. It cost me about $135.00 to fix it. I was so glad that no cars were in the lot.

The brakes fluid line broke. It was an older car and my husband said I should have thrown it into reverse and only damaged the transmission.

My daughter Sandi rolled over in a friend's car one night. I gave her some free time at three p.m. while I did the laundry and shopped for groceries. I told her I'd pick her up at 6 p.m. I didn't see her until lunch time the next day. The kids said they didn't know which way to go after the car stopped rolling over in the country.

My daughter's teacher said that was the best excuse for being late was this one. The friend's raccoon that was in the car pushed the door buttons down and they couldn't get back in the car to go to school. Well they say truth is stranger than fiction!

We watched a funny one one day. Watching from the laundry window, we saw a boy try to drive threw a large snow bank. What he didn't know was, it was a lot of ice, from a previous storm. He got stuck on top of it with no wheels on the ground. They had to tow his four wheel drive off the snow bank.

I went down the hill and almost ran into three boulders on my side of the road. I knew a big truck was behind me and I couldn't see very far ahead due to fog. I dashed around the boulders and hoped no one was in the opposing lane of traffic. It was scary! I drove nine miles to the gas station to report the incident close to Big Bear Lake.

My Dawna graduated from Big Bear High School.

She was serving at a luncheon at school one day when one of the guys at one table started bugging her. He did it once too often, and my daughter came back with a cup of coffee and poured it on him. I said "You didn't". She said "I did" – he asked for it! I got a laugh out of it. His girlfriend started laughing, so no harm done.

My daughter brought me a package of Clairol hair dye just before graduation. A hint to me. It worked I dyed my hair for the first time.

Dawna told me you don't want the top jock to date. Too stuck on himself, next one down better – will pay more attention to you.

Here's a funny one involving Sandy. She went down the hill to a vet one day to have her dogs' ears clipped. She came home laughing and said guess what the vet used to hold up the dogs ears – the cardboard part of a tampax.

111

I read this one someplace. A guy was working on his roof.

r safety he decided to tie himself to his car on the opposite side

roof. His wife got into their car and took off – pulling him off

e roof. – Ouch!

I let Dawna (daughter) go to the Colorado River, where the

m is. A friend's mother drove there. After she came home

meone said "Guess what she did?" She won the Wet-T-Shirt

ntest. A shocked mom I said "What? I didn't know they did

ings like that." She had a good figure.

A special tip for mountain driving – so your brakes don't overheat,

ar down part of the time coming down on a mountain road.

14) Small House

Our family broke up and I moved into small house in B. B. Lake

Wall down

Carpet

Puppy (Joey)

Oven

Hair cut

Snow tips

We moved into another small house in Big Bear Lake. We had a bad snow storm and looked out at our car, it was buried. A small child climbed on the snow pile and my Wally said to the mother "Would you like to take your son off my continental?' She said 'Oh!' And moved him.

Just before this storm we had to lay a piece of carpet upside down in the road to mark it for cutting with string and blue chalk. It worked, no traffic. Small street. Backyard was too muddy.

Our little house needed kitchen shelves so we put in open shelves, that helped and the carpet I found was beautiful golden brown thick shag for the living room.

We asked the landlord to ok tearing down a non-retaining wall so we could lay carpeting. He never answered. We tore it down. It made the house look much better.

114

While still in small house my Wally asked if I'd like a puppy. He went to pick him up. He put him on the car seat and a little later, sat in the mess. He came in laughing. Little Joey was so tiny I couldn't get mad at him. We decided to keep him. His adult weight was eight pounds. He was a peek-a-poo tan color but with a poodle head. He played ball with a tennis ball. A Pekinese couldn't do it, he has a short nose.

Oven blew up when lighting it one day and burnt my bangs. Went for a hair cut some time later, the girl cut it wrong and I took down mirrors in the house so I wouldn't have to look at it, and the girl got fired that cut it.

I learned a few things about snow.

1) Park your car in aimed down hill direction if a storm is coming in.

2) Leave room for the plow to get by.

3) Drive with chains on, 15 to 25 miles per hour. Gear down

115

to 15 miles per hour before trying to stop.

4) Landlord called me and asked me to clear ice off the gas meter. It was sitting right under the icicles coming off the roof. He only called me when big storm hit one and half foot overnight snow. A tiny roof was over the meter.

5) A friend told me if your sliding glass door sticks you need to clear snow off your roof. Rafters are starting to bend.

6) I also learned to get out of my driveway before two hours of snow, it was uphill a little.

7) My kids learned how to make quick money taking off chains at $5.00 a crack for the flatlanders that didn't know how to do it.

8) You must have chains in your car trunk, not broken, ready to put on, at the start of the storm, if a cop stops you.

9) They now make heated driveways for houses on hills.

10) To make snow cream for family to eat, use clean snow. rich milk or cream, sugar and vanilla. Pour over snow.

Chapter 15

Desert

Experiences

p. 117

15) My Desert Experience

Caretaking ghost town

Snakes

Dog fight

P. O. Box

Tumbleweeds

Fire

Sun poisoning

High heels

Drunk

Dehydration

Animals in pen

Killer dog

Marriage

Rain storm

Joey's mouse

Broom chase

Drunk spiders

Lucerne Valley goose

Psychic

Surgery

Desert tips

Rex

We got tired of Big Bear snow. We moved down to Apple Valley which is high desert at about 3,500 feet. Palm Springs is low desert below sea level, good for winters, constant air conditioners for summer.

In high desert I discovered swamp coolers. They run on water.

We owned a camper truck so we had an instant house to live in. It was something to park beside the ghost town buildings which were empty rooms in the desert. Upon further checking we found they would let us use one of the rooms to live in.

Living on a small pension check my Wally and I moved to a job caretaking a ghost town near Apple Valley, California. It gave us free rent. We stayed two years at "Dead Mans Point".

We played around at the local swap meet for fun and learned how to buy and sell.

Being in the desert I saw my first (three) snakes. They like to hide and cool off under rocks. I was warned to stay away from the shady side of rocks. I also got a warning about green snakes, stay away from them, poisonous like a rattlesnake. The owners son brought down from the rock pile a "king" snake. He had the head in one hand and the tail in the other hand and it was laying across his shoulders. His Dad was there and said "take it away." To which his son said "It's ok Dad he eats the rattlesnakes. One green snake came inside the chain link fence. I had a guy chase him away and he went right through the fence.

The owner's family came out to the property to ride their dirt bikes. Even though they are quite dangerous.

I got so hot one day I picked up the water hose and drowned me with it.

One day a guest of the owner brought his dog with him and it got in a fight with our German shepherd watch dog. Mine was protecting his property.

We wanted a P. O. Box, but we hit a snag there. They wanted an address first. We didn't have one so had to think about it. We were living in the middle of the desert and had no address. We had to go to a realtor to figure it out.

Another thing I found out about desert living is you need a simple hair-do for the wind.

Drinking too much beer at the swap meet Wally, my husband, bought too high and sold too low. Not good.

A caretaker was needed because people were starting to tear off part of the building, they wanted the old wood. They also took his stove, so he built one that couldn't be moved.

One thing that was cute in the desert was done with tumbleweeds. They stack up three of them in different sizes. They spray paint them white and have a cute snowman.

We had a fire one night a couple of hills away from us. I called the fire department and they said – they were on it, one said "It was a rude awakening wasn't it?" I said yes and hung up the phone. Then we watched the fire 'til about 2 a.m. When I was sure their firebreak would work and stop it, I went to bed.

One day my little dog got a tumble weed stuck on him. My German shepherd looked at him and grabbed it with his teeth and pulled it off, a few days later he did it again. He was taking care of his little brother, Joey.

I laid out in the sun one day and got sun poisoning in 40 minutes. I only intended to stay 20 minutes, should have turned over! I had face and arms under a tree, luckily. It got me good, I was in a bikini.

A nurse told me to get off my feet. My circulation was bad. Fix a pot of tea, dip white towels in it and lay them on me for a week. I slept on a plastic lounge chair. I also took water pills once a day at 2 p.m. I came out of it ok. Glad my arms and face were under a tree! The tannic acid in tea helped.

I learned in the desert high heels sink in the sand. A high
wedge is better, need thick rubble sole. I also learned you get
sand in your eyes. Eye doctors do well! Also the desert areas
have shoe repair shops. The sand wears off the sole of your
shoes, like sandpaper.

My husband drove home one day and parked outside the gate.
He was too drunk to drive through it. It was a double gate.

In the desert dehydration can be a problem, as my husband
found out one day. He suddenly felt strange. A nearby ex nurse
gave him specific directions. Put some butter on a slice of bread,
sprinkle a bunch of salt on it. Eat it and drink a large glass of water.
He came out of it ok.

We had a bunch of tumbleweeds pile up in front of our gate
one day, thought we'd have to find a pitchfork to remove them.
Woke up the next morning to find the wind had blown them all
away.

Watch babies. They need liquid too.

The owners brought out their malamute-husky to be friends with our dog, "Rex". They did ok together – but he taught my dog to crawl under the fence and escape. They didn't have sense enough to come back in the same way they got out and would always wait by the front gate to be let back in.

The owner's dog was a little wild. We got in a few small animals for the grandchildren to see and put them in a separate small fenced area. We had two goats, two turkeys and two ducks. One day we busted up laughing watching the duck trying to teach the turkey how to swim. One day the goats started pulling tail feathers out of the turkeys and the goat ate the food bag. The bag was paper.

Another day we had a scare. At 5 a.m. the malamute mix figured out how to open the animal gate and attacked the goat. He killed it, one at least. Then someone yelled, where's the other goat. We ran around the building and found him on top of our car hood. My husband chased him and ran to a stairway that went onto the roof. My husband had to chase him back down which was cute. We learned that this type of dog will kill but won't eat its prey.

We got married in the desert while we were there at Dead Man's Point. A western wedding with jean western shirts, cowboy hat, etc.

I drove to the city of Orange one day. Upon returning to Apple Valley I had a problem. A large dark cloud was hanging over San Bernardino five miles ahead of me. It would be a quick trip through that area so I continued to drive. A large mistake! It let loose as I hit the area. I couldn't see it was coming down so hard. I chose to get off the freeway. I passed a small car that had flooded out on the off ramp and drove off ramp to regular streets and they had about a foot of water on them. I asked a guy walking how it was where he'd been and he said forget it. I then chose to drive to higher ground and parked my car in a restaurant parking lot that was much higher ground and sat for two hours. Then drove home. Worst rainstorm I've ever been in.

125

Joey, my little (eight pound) dog had a cute little story. He was chasing a little mouse around the room. I didn't know he had a nest in my desk! – A board was missing in the back of the desk. He leaned out of the drawer and yelled at my Joey, for chasing him. You could barely hear him. He was mad!

I rented a motel room on the beach one time. The manager gave me a mouse trap and put peanut butter on it. It worked.

Another thing happened while in Apple Valley. We had just put a couple of steaks on the bar-b-q. Suddenly my German shepherd discovered the steaks. Our dog got too close and my husband went after him with a broom.

Another incident was this. A German guy didn't like spiders and they were in his house. He had the bug man spray his house and around all baseboards. When asked if it worked he answered: "The spiders are drunk and staggering around now."

126

We then moved our trailer onto another property in Lucerne Valley. We stayed about a year. One of the owner's children said "I don't like the goose that lives here." I thought what's so bad about the goose? Then one day I was walking along and turned around to find a goose with his head down deliberately aimed at me at running speed. The child was right!!

I had another experience while living there. I went to see a psychic. It cost $25.00 for 30 minutes at that time. He also made a cassette of the interview which I got. That was 15 years ago.

He started out by telling me I lived in a trailer. Said I was debating my life. Which I was. Said I had just met someone, which I had. Told me he's a Pisces horoscope. Which he was. Said I was contemplating a trip. Which I was. Told me I would take the trip but I would come back. He said "He's got money." I said which one. He said "you're husband"! I thought to myself you're kidding. He hadn't shown me anything so far. We had

127

very little money. An interesting visit.

I took the trip East to Michigan and Ohio, visiting his family and my Dad. We stayed in northern Michigan one year.

I lined up a surgery appointment at George Air Base for two months later. I used the property owner's phone. The base called me and said surgery would be one month later. The owner didn't tell me. I was very shocked walking into the base hospital and being told it would be a month later. I burst into tear and went home.

This one is a construction story. A lady's husband built a house in the desert. She came out to see the house. She found a snake on her porch. Went back home and told him to sell it.

Desert tips:

1) There is a poisonous brown spider.

2) Boots shake twice, bang it to check for spiders.

3) Keep your doors shut to keep out the creepy crawlers.

4) Look over your doorway, a large snake could be curled up

round it. They could also be under shade trees.

5) Clear bushes from sidewalk area, to see better.

6) A three story A frame house may be too tall for strong
desert winds.

7) Ladies high heels sink in the sand, better to wear a high
heel wedge shoe.

I had one bad experience in Lucerne Valley one day. My
German shepherd didn't come home. I put an ad in the paper and
described him perfectly. He had a broken front tooth, a split on
both ears and perfect German shepherd coloring. Disposition
terrific! A lady called me and said "I have your dog. I'll bring
him back Friday." That was two days later. His name was Rex.
She never showed up. That was years ago. I still miss him.

If someone asked you would you admit to having a one night
stand. Yes – and was it worth it. Yes – I have my memories and
have never forgotten it. It made me feel like maybe someone might
want me after what my husband put me through.

16) Michigan Trip

Trip to Vegas and back

Trip East by bus

Michigan apartment

Icicles and Joey

Rose pinecones

Apartment near bar

Very few apartments available

Fall on ice

Don't leave Joey

Joey's treats

Dad's house - Ohio

Before leaving for Michigan my husband built a bed into the

back of our van. We took a trip to Las Vegas first. I thought we were

coming back. We got into an argument and he put me in a cab and

went to the bus station. He followed for a ways – then stopped.

continued to the station. I waited a couple of hours to see if he

would come and talk to me. I then bought a bus ticket home. I

came into the Victorville station and paid a cab driver to take me

out to the main road. I was running out of money so I hitchhiked

home to Lucerne Valley. Three rides were offered me. The first

one took me to the edge of town. The second one offered a ride.

looked inside the car and said, "No thank you"! He didn't have

stitch of clothes on. Someone asked me later what color the car was

and I answered I can't remember, a light color. I was so shocked I

didn't remember. My third ride was a friend and she took me the

rest of the way home.

My husband drove from Vegas to Michigan alone except for my

little dog Joey. He was a Pekinese-poodle mix. He told me later he

liked chicken nuggets from McDonalds. After arriving in Michigan my husband called me.

I took a bus ride to Michigan from California. One night the driver stopped the bus because it broke down and we had to wait for a new bus. It picked us up after five hours of waiting about two a.m. The driver said he stopped because he didn't think it was a very good idea to wind up in the Colorado River.

I arrived in Michigan with $2.00 left. I started out with $20.00 for food. So I did all right.

They had one too many on the bus at one town. So they took me off and put me on a bus going through Wisconsin. I went all the way to the top of state and crossed a bridge into Michigan.

I found out it isn't even safe on a bus. I met a flasher on the second seat. I pushed my seat forward and didn't turn around again.

I had to get what was left of my belongings into storage before leaving to join my husband. He wired me bus money.

We got a small apartment in Indian River, Michigan. The refrigerat in it must have been the first one made after the icebox. Did not work well. The apartment was upstairs.

The winter icicles got so long we had to have them knocked off, they were dangerous over the apartment doorway.

My little dog Joey was so cute. I thought I'd take his picture in the picture window above my couch. It was covered with icicles. I set him up on the back of the couch to snap the picture and the icicles fell down. The timing was perfect. I didn't get the picture.

I gathered some tiny rose pinecones from the trees nearby when I got bored in the apartment. I thought I could make something out of them.

Spending money before you cash your pension check, its not the way to do it! My husband ran up a bar bill for $300 one month in Michigan.

We stayed there for a year, in a one bedroom apartment. My husband picked it out – half block from a bar. I think he did it so he could walk home and leave his car there, if he was too drunk to drive. There's very few apartments in Indian River, Michigan.

133

I fell on ice there and had to see a chiropractor. He told me to lay down and use ice on my back, don't walk. He gave me an elastic brace for my back and said use it every time you have to get up. He put me back in place.

The chiropractor told me to put several wet washcloths into zip lock baggies and freeze them. They're flat to lay on with back injury, a good ice pack. They also will bend around other types of injury.

When we were packing our van my little dog Joey watched for a while, then jumped in the van and wouldn't leave it. Like he knew we were leaving Michigan and he didn't want to be left behind.

Every time he went to grandma's house he made a beeline for his dish in the corner. A treat from Grandma, she loved him too! He loved his milk bones dog biscuits and hid them under the wall heater or behind my couch pillows. He always knew where to find them.

We visited my Dad in Ohio for about a week, then my husband just took off and left me, saying I was sick. My Mother was called and she sent me a plane ticket home. When she saw me she said I wasn't well and took me home to Colorado.

My storage was in California. It had been there for a year. My sister went to pick up my things and found water damage. It must have come in under the door, a bad storm they said. It ruined half my things. My sister put my remainder of things in her garage.

While in Marion, Ohio I found many changes there. The house grew up in was white, its now painted bright yellow and dark brown. So I didn't want to take a picture of it.) Ugh!

My ice cream store had many broken windows in it, closed down for good.

My supermarket where I had worked had burned down.

My skating rink had been torn down.

A sad remembrance of my hometown of 35,000 people, my high school had 1,500 students.

I wrote my Dad one day while living in Big Bear and said "I went down the hill." He wrote back and said "I thought you lived on a mountain".

When I went to Michigan they had their own way of talking. It was "down state or upstate", if you asked where they were going.

Did I tell you my local ice cream store was a little different? They didn't use an ice cream dipper. They used a spatula. It was pointed. They put it twice into tub of ice cream and placed a mountain of ice cream onto the cone. More fun to eat that way.

17) Mother

    Hawaii – volcano

    Estes Park

    Lightening

    Accident

    Animals

    Stanley Hotel

    Perfume

    Stepfather Charles

    Joshua

    Diamond rings

    Snowman

    Car died

    Blood scare

    Ketchup – uncle

    Raccoon

    Boy doll

Van in lake

Grandson visit

She had a few experiences worth talking about.

She lived in Hawaii almost two years. She walked around the volcano edge on another island – had to stay on path – it erupted the next day! Oops!

She had a papaya tree. In trying to pick the fruit she had a problem. The lizards kept trying to crawl up her legs. She solved it. She got some rubber bands and put them around her pant legs. A native came by and said "you no like papaya?" She showed him her refrigerator. It was full. Told him to take all he wanted.

Every chance they got they swam at Waikiki Beach. The water is warm and clear.

When my Mother left Hawaii she carried in her car trunk coconuts for the grandchildren. She bought a wood burning set to put names and dates on all of them.

She found out that food and rent were expensive. Also they don't use stuffed furniture in Hawaii. Just foam because of the humidity being so high there. Things will mildew. Had to spray books and leave light on in closet all night to help dry out clothes. Also had to spray kitchen every day to keep cockroaches out.

It takes two years to grow a pineapple in Hawaii.

She was sitting on the hearth of her fireplace downstairs, when lightening hit the top of her chimney and broke it off. The fire trucks came flying up her hill to see who got hit. It didn't hurt her, and no fire. She thought an airplane hit her house.

My Mother had one accident driving into Estes Park on ice. They hadn't put the dirt on the road yet. She slid off the hill and hit a tree and the car dropped straight down onto some rocks. She wasn't hurt this time either. Luck was with her. She was driving a big white cadallac. A classic, but it was ruined.

My Mother had two baby deer playing her yard one day, three days old, thought they were twins at first. Two moms had babies on the same day. No pictures. They wouldn't sit still. In Estes Park you live among the animals.

One day two black squirrels played running up and down her trees. Not allowed to shoot them, an endangered species. One day was scary. A huge herd of big elk came around both sides of the house. They could have jumped through her living room window, it happened to some one before. Don't remember where.

My Mother told me this one. The old Stanley Hotel in Estes Park has this story. Mr. Stanley did not know how to turn around his Stanley steamer car. So – he put a turntable in his garage. All he had to do was drive in and push a button to turn around.

My stepfather did a cute one one day. He wrote to a perfume company to complain that no perfume was in his favorite store and why wasn't it there? They sent him two bottles of my Mother's favorite perfume free.

My stepfather was a "flying tiger" during the war, he flew in China, Burma and India. Then switched to a an air traffic controller o.

141

My stepfather Charles started selling cars on the side. He got so good at it, he had to hire another salesman to complete his deals. The boss decided he didn't quite know how he did it. He brought his wife in to check up on him, she came in as a customer. After dealing with Charles she said "He's good – I'd buy from him too!"

One day a bird flew into their fireplace in Estes Park and got stuck inside the screen. Mother called a neighbor for help. He said, "I'm afraid of birds call somebody else."

My Mother had a cute little neighbor boy names Joshua. He came over one day and knocked on her door. He was three years old and said "My mother said I can't come in unless you ask me." My Mother said "Do you want to come in?" He nodded. He walked all over the house and came back and said "You have a very comfortabl house." He visited my Mother many times. She went to Grandma's Day at school. His grandma was too far away.

He came in the door one day and took off his shoes. My Mother said "I'll bet you have another pair of socks just like that one." He

.ked down at his different colors and said "I couldn't find the mates"
l "what's the difference any way!"

This is a story my Mother told me. A lady friend went to take a
»wer. Took off her rings and put them in a kleenex. She placed
m on the top of the toilet tank. Her husband came into the bathroom,
v the kleenex and thought it didn't belong there. He picked it up
l threw it into the toilet and flushed it. No more rings. They called
plumber, but didn't find the rings.

Another friend came to visit one day and had saran wrapped around
· glasses. She was trying to keep the pollen out of her eyes. She was
:rgic to everything.

One year we went to Grandma's for a visit. The children were
appointed, no snow! We drove out to where the beavers live and
nd enough snow to make a snowman. My Mother looked at him
a minute. Then opened the car trunk and we put each section in
car trunk. We drove it home and put him on the patio and put him
·k together. Mission accomplished!

143

This is a cute story – true. A couple living on the mountain wanted to go to a dance that was down the mountain. It started snowing. They decided to go anyway. As they started up the hill, they got about three blocks up and the car died. No battery power either. They found a flashlight. The girls decided they didn't want to ruin their long dresses. So, they took them off! – put their coats back on. They walked down the mountain to a house, to make a phone call to tow their car. The guy said you must be cold and put them by the fireplace. It took a while to get the tow truck there. The guy came back to them and said "You still have your coats on, I'll turn up the heat." What he didn't know was they couldn't take their coats off with nothing on underneath. Then one of the girls suddenly noticed something was wrong. She had no bra on. Maybe it came off with her dress. They got back to their car and looked for it. No bra! The story went to several lodges and the girls started getting packages. The first was a trainer bra. And many more followed!!

This story happened in Estes Park. A truck parked in front of the corner coffee shop downtown. The driver went inside. A lady saw blood under the truck and thought maybe he killed somebody and called the police. They came out to check the situation out. Found he had killed a deer, out of season and with out license. I don't know the penalty for this crime, probably a fine. Plus, they told him he would never be allowed to hunt here again. They would not give him a hunting license.

I have an uncle that was in the service and said to a waitress I can eat ketchup on anything." She got a piece of chocolate cake nd put ketchup on it and said eat it!

A friend of Mothers had a raccoon in her basement. She was one for three days and came back to find him there. She called meone to get help. He said how long has he been there? Answering ree days, he knew what to do. He put food on each step of the airway and walked him out the door.

145

I have an Aunt Ruby that got a gift from my Mother one day. It was an anatomically correct little boy doll. My Mother said, "Here's the little boy you never had." Upon which my Aunt said "I'll have some fun with him." She took him to her doctor (who was a baby doctor) and put him in a baby blanket. She was in the baby ward of the hospital. She waited for the doctor to come in. Then she said to him "I thought you said I wasn't pregnant!" She threw off the blanket and said, "and it's a boy". The doctor was so startled he jumped backwards a step.

Another Estes Park story happened on the fourth of July a few years ago. We were across the lake from where the fireworks were going to go off. All of a sudden we heard a big commotion. After talking to some people we found out what it was. Some guy in a van drove into the lake. He hit several people on the way in and was in three feet of water. We had police and a "water rescue van". I think they took him away, he was probably drunk.

146

Here's another story – a grandson, 17 years old, wanted to come

a visit to Colorado. He had long hair. He called Grandma, she

d "First you have to cut your hair." He arrived later and said "What

ne do I have to come in Grandma?" Answer – twelve midnight.

said "why Grandma?" She said "because, I won't worry about

u after twelve and if you're late you will be on the next plane home!"

spent the summer with Grandma and Grandpa.

Grandpa suggested he go into the Air Force if he wanted to join a

litary service. He did and later became a member of the special

ces Air Force group, specializing in parachute jumping, helicopter

cue. Two stories follow.

1) A fisherman radioed in SOS, mayday boat capsized. A helicopter

s sent out with a three man rescue, eight foot waves in the ocean.

ey found him. They got him ready to go up into the copter with

e man helping him. The pilot suddenly called down – shark in the

ter and my nephew yelled up, hurry up because he was still waiting.

ary! He made it!

147

2) A Russian ship radioed medical emergency. My nephew was helicoptered to ship. He decided it was an appendicitis attack and operated. He stayed five days on ship to make sure he was ok. Then someone asked - "What if he'd died?" To which he answered – "They'd probably shoot me."

The P. J.'s jumped out over Niagara Falls once just to prove how good they are. That was dangerous too!

My nephew has done so well. The family is very proud of him.

My Mother said there were two things she missed from early years in Marion, Ohio. The early harvest apple tree in backyard of neighbors house – (we all shared it) and – the Isaly's Ice Cream store with its mountain shaped cones. I said me too.

18) My Time with Mom

Storage problems

Alzheimer's

Suitcase

Spelling problems

Walking to count of three

Laundry

Jail

Spring Creek

Photo album

Recipe cards

Boyfriend incident

Doctor

After arriving in Estes Park I told my Mother I had storage in Apple Valley, California. They got me to sign a paper allowing my sister to take my things to her garage. – And guess what? They had a bad rain storm and my things were damaged and mildewed in the paid storage that I had for one year. I lost half of my things. My sister's garage – the roof leaked and I lost a few more things – darn! My luck seemed to be all bad.

My Mother took good care of me for seven years. After taking me to many doctors, they diagnosed me with Alzheimer's disease. My Mother said "no it can't be, she is too young." They put me on vitamins and such saying I was very run down physically. I got emotionally upset and they put me on haldol but I got worse and they took me off of it. – After I got mad at my Mother in the car one day, I reached for the door but didn't jump out. I was furious because my Mother got rid of all my things in my suitcase that I had brought with me and she threw my luggage out. Too! I liked it! It was nice merican tourister "white" fiber glass with quilted red satin lining,

four piece set.

The doctor put me in the hospital to gradually pull me off haldol

:dication. Said I was allergic to it.

I had a problem writing down things and reversing a couple of

ters spelling things wrong. I don't know what that was all about.

I also did something else that was strange for awhile. I sat down

unted to three and got up and walked a bit. Don't know what

used that either.

One day in Estes Park we went to the laundry. Upon leaving I

:ked up a few old magazines. My Mother had a fit. She freaked

t in the car, caused enough commotion to have a lady cop come by

d told the cop I hit her, which I didn't! She'd lived in town for

ars and knew everybody. I was new in town so they believed her.

ey put me in jail overnight. I still haven't forgiven her for that

e. I didn't touch her.

151

My Mother had her hands full taking care of me. After seven
years she put me into a nursing home called Spring Creek Health
Care in Fort Collins, Colorado. That's been quite an experience.
I've now been here for ten years. Many people have come and gone,
and that includes the residents and the help. I had no place better
to go to. I have now moved four times in the building. Once because
they were redecorating and changed the unit I was living in. Other
times to change roommates.

I fixed a small photo album just of Spring Creek, for my memories.

I've also fixed six recipe boxes, the four by six size so there's room
for pictures of what you're cooking. I always wanted to do that. I had
to do something to keep my head busy and keep my sanity. All pictures
came from magazines donated to us. I glued them on, weighting them
down under a heavy box overnight so the cards won't curl up. Elmer's
glue worked well. It was fun.

152

Spring Creek provides many activities to help pass the time away,

e bingo, social gatherings and snacks, music entertainers and a once

month birthday party. We also go to Walmart shopping once a week.

After leaving Estes Park to live off the mountain daughter Marilyn

gested "change churches to one in Loveland, Colorado" and meet

neone ten years younger than you. So he'll be able to keep up with

. A while later Mother said "I have a friend he's six feet tall has

ite wavy hair. He's an ex "banker" - suggesting he had money. After

ouple of months she showed us an engagement ring. The story went

for a year and a half. She never introduced him to any of the family.

ally the children couldn't stand it anymore and suggested coming

on Easter Sunday to go to church with Mother to meet him. She said

was seeing him in church every week. So Mother decided things

gone far enough. She then said "I made it all up there is no such

friend! My children shouldn't tell me who I should go out with,

uld they?"

153

My Mother has a sense of humor doesn't she? She bought a
zirconium ring to make story more real.

What's that saying, "I don't get mad I get even"!

Mother said to her doctor one day. "With this type of exam – don't
you think we should be on a first name basis?" The doctor cracked up an
later with her bill wrote his name on it in very large letters at the bottom.

I commented that my Mother's weight was still the same – she said –
"It's rearranged itself a little bit."

19) Spring Creek

Flood

Thompson

Comments

Doris

Doctor test

Halloween

My doctor

Corin and Wendel

Beauty operator

Second hand store

Martha and Anna

Dominoes

Swat team

Fire

Recipes

MRI and test

George

Mice

Still sane

Surprise phone call 2005

Roller skates

Back problems

Daddy's comment

Marriage comments

First off we survived the 1998 Spring Creek flood because we are up on a hill. It happened at night. I walked across the bridge the next morning at about ten a.m. Most of the water had gone down. It did damage, four houses deep, on the other side of the river. It was the low side. A guy told me a Volkswagen was under water when it hit the parking lot across the street, on LeMay. The second house lucked out. The triple garage had water in it. But their overhead apartment was ok. The third house a lady was sweeping water out her front door. Forth house did the same.

Ninety trailers on corner of College and Stuart were damaged. They were downhill from the road.

Queen Elizabeth of England sent $1,000,000 to the flood victims. It comes out to about $10,000 per family. One visitor said she lived along the river and the water came to within one foot of her front door.

It rained eight inches in four hours. Thompson canyon flood twenty years ago was twelve inches in four hours.

Thompson Canyon flood stories:

1) A man cooking on outside bar-b-q looked up and saw the swirling water rising in the river. Called to his wife twice! She came out, they looked at the water. Jumped into their car and headed across the bridge. A man was screaming in the water. He was badly hurt, they pulled him into the car and headed for a nearby road that climbed up the hill. They applied a tourniquet to the man's leg and sat all night on the hill.

2) One lady heard on C. B. radio that something was happening in the canyon. She drove into the lower end of canyon to save her son, even though warned to not enter. The water took her husband out of the car and the wife yelled "It's the end of the world" into the C.B. and it took her too.

3) A bus driver started into lower end of canyon, thought the water didn't look good. Turned around and left. He saved a bus load of kids.

4) Two people were sleeping along the river in sleeping bags.

They couldn't get out of their sleeping bags and drowned.

5) The water was 35 feet deep at the bottom of the canyon.

6) The water destroyed seven houses in a row in one section.

Its sometimes sad and some times funny as you listen to the comments around you living in a nursing home. I walked by Dwight, a tall six foot gentleman and he kiddingly said "Trip why don't you", to which I answered "I hope not", as I continued across the dining room.

Another day Charlie said "I'm glad I didn't get diabetes or arthritis". I thought about who said it for a minute. He's 103 years old, and has lost his hearing and eyesight.

One day a guy said "I'm just waiting for her to take off her shirt', as he looked at me.   A kitchen help girl said upon hearing him "You're only allowed to say that to your wife!"

On another day, a CNA said "Get your hands off my ass!" to the same guy. You could hear her clear across the room.

159

One wife came in and said her four sons call her and say "This is your favorite son." Which one????

Several women were caught walking down the hallway missing her pants, and underwear too. They were then moved to Alzheimer's wing.

One guy had his artificial eye thrown away – how awful.

One year we had a nice lady named Doris, a resident, age 92. She gave me a white fabric dove. I decided to make a bunch of them for Christmas and I gave two to everyone on my list. I told Doris where I sent them, N. H., California, Ohio etc. and she said "Well I was good for something!" She was about 93 years old.

Lunch was a little bit late one day. "When do we eat?" someone said. "Foods coming", another one said. Charlie said "So's Christmas

Doctor test (Barium enema) hospital March – 2001.

Doctor came in and said I hear you have a "little" problem – I said "What do you mean little?"

To anyone it will help to wear to the test loose stretchy pants and ong top to cover up. You will come home in a diaper. I accidentally lid it right! Intestinal tests are awful.

One day I went upstairs to mail a letter and couldn't lick the stamp. hen I asked the nurse if the medicine caused reaction and she said es. Dry mouth.

Halloween ideas – costumes

1) Large clear trash bag to wear from neck to thigh. Fill with right colored balloons to look like jelly beans.

2) One took her electric car and made it look like a Flintstone car.

3) One group of adults made a flag. Everyone dressed in white. ll had red stripes except one. He did the blue with star square. On e they made the flag wave.

All are original ideas.

At a later date they did a bone density test – I flunked the test. It ld me I had a bone problem. I finally found out why my lower back

161

hurt. I wish they'd found out sooner.

I've tried to read up on what things help a bone problem.

I've studied two books "Lets Eat Right to Keep Fit" by Adelle Dav
and "Vitamin Bible" by Earl Mindell. They're both paperback books,
white with red lettering around $7.00 each.

One little lady named Corin was in the television lounge one day.
I asked if she wanted something, she said she "didn't know".

I am going to take a picture of Wendel, a sweet guy, a college
chemistry teacher. He looks like Grandpa from the cover of Post
Magazine years ago, like the Saturday Evening Post.

We've had a lot of good people working here.

When one of the girls went to her beauty operator and was told
she was pulling her hair too tight into ponytail type hair do, told to
stop it, it must be looser. Her hair was falling out along the hair line!

You don't have a lot of money if you're living in a nursing home.

I started shopping in second hand stores, after one girl told me where e was. I then looked them up in the phone book and got addresses of ıers.

A little lady named Martha met my Mother and always had a estion for me. "How's your Mother?" every time I went by.

We've had a dominoes game going every Monday evening for ew years. Its fun!

We had one girl here that was epileptic. She played dominoes with She got permission from her doctor and Mother to go to work and ık the bus to quick food place. She moved away later and we missed r, her name was Anna.

A Spring Creek situation when an irate relative said he was coming to take a patient out. The person had a gun. The swat team and police ne in. The C.N.A.s ordered everyone into their rooms. Things calmed wn after a little while. They talked to the guy.

163

A smoking patient set himself on fire in the smoking room one day. The fire department was called. He lived three hours. Now no smoking is allowed inside the building.

My interest in writing this book started at Spring Creek Health Care Center. After we discussed a few things that happened in my life someone said "Why don't you write a book" -- "you've had an interesting life." It happened three or four times, so I was gradually talked into the idea.

Another idea to use up my time started me doing this: I started cutting out "pictures" of recipes and gluing them and recipes onto four by six recipe cards. I much prefer seeing a picture of what I'm going to make. I now have five boxes finished and I'm going to quit.

I'm now pushing to finish my book!

I was put into Spring Creek Nursing Home years ago because of a diagnosis of Alzheimer.

My friend, Greta, recommended retesting me. After doing a

mplete neurological testing which took five and half hours the test

dy agreed. No Alzheimer! Showed on testing – and she agreed to

commend the MRI test be done again, for comparison to first one

hich my Mother saw. Alzheimer diagnosis was a mistake. It was

ne seventeen years ago.

I just re-did the MRI test again – and guess what they found. I

ve two small cysts in my head. They could cause small personality

anges. Doctor said it may have been caused from a head injury I

ceived when I was about 22 years old. I had a concussion then. The

ow was to the upper center of forehead. I had a good lump on my

ad. After one week with a slight headache the doctor said now put

at on it. I did. I went into my uncle's swimming pool at 90 degrees.

e lump went down the next day and I had two black eyes for another

ek. I had melted the blood clot and it ran downhill.

One story from Spring Creek was sad. My tablemate George went

work one day and didn't return that night. He was working part

e at Walmart and was riding the bus back and forth. After checking with the driver found he was on the bus that day. Two children found him in a near by lake five days later.

Mice, ugh! I could have gone all my life without this incident.

One lady resident moved into my room. I didn't know she was not neat. She had food crumbs in her large recliner chair and in her drawers. They decided to replace her old chair and pulled it out of the room. Five or six mice ran in all directions. It took us several days to catch them with mousetraps. Yuck!

I gave my Mother part of my book to read – she said "You can't write a book that way." My sister also said "What makes you think anyone will buy your book?"

I said – thinking positive – "What makes you think they won't?"

Negative people are depressing. Betty Browning gave me positive feedback – and named my book after reading some of it.

This came down in 2005. I wrote to a friend in Big Bear Lake area

see where "Wally" was, years after being in Colorado, because of my

ness. His letters were found after he died, by his sister. So she knew

here I was.

In a nursing home for ten years I got a surprise call from his sister

Florida, in August of 2004.

Mary called me and said "Are you still married to him?" I said yes

which she said, "Go for the benefits." He died three months ago!"

e was 71 years old and died of lung and brain cancer.

In order to straighten things out legally, I now needed my marriage

ense and his death certificate – and as I found out later also had to

ove first marriage and divorce and his first marriage and divorce.

In past years my Mother lost my important papers.

I thought about it and called information long distance and a

cording said "If your marriage was confidential go to county records,

t the state. I said ok. They sent me a paper I had to notarize it and

nd it back with money.

167

In 2005 I wanted to leave Spring Creek. My second husband had died and left me with a military pay check. It took about nine months to straighten out the paper work and line up a Social Security check from my first husband also.

I located an apartment but was told I couldn't leave Spring Creek. Guardian said, "no." Darn it. I was ready. They forced me to sign a paper saying I would stay. They said they would call the police on me if I left. My positive thinking didn't work. I was shocked! I thought my life was over. I didn't know they had that much control over me.

My second husband's death was caused by Agent Orange in Viet Nam and gave him cancer years later. I got a monthly check of $1000 as his wife.

My first husband gave me Social Security check as his wife of over ten years.

I got a sudden retroactive large check amout from each husband when the paper work was done, and bought a new television, stereo $300 and sewing machine $600. That was nice.

I was asked this one, "You've been in a nursing home ten years and you're not crazy yet?" Answer, "I try to think to a positive future."

Now they think I can leave, after taking away my money. Cute, huh? All I wanted was my financial security that I was entitled to.

The mental stress has been terrific!

I've caught more than mistake with those handling my money. Its a good thing I pay attention to details.

At one point I decided to get some roller skates and go for some exercise at the rink again. Big mistake, I fell down the third time out. Since I have osteoporosis, a very bad idea, I am now trying to sell my ska My skates I lost in storage damage were much better quality anyway.

money came down from Veterans and I boug a television, stereo, sewing machine and camera, fun but hectic, had thirt days to do it in.

The food here is bland, to serve 150 people, little seasoning. They serve on a budget of $4.00 per person per day. Hard to believe.

Grandma Turner had spina bifida baby – died at eight months.

From fall on ice in Michigan I now have a vertebra that slips out of place. They did an MRI of my lower back. The report came back with this, a missing vertebra and disc. I said what? Doctor said you have four should have five below the waist. You could have been an inch or two

169 ½

taller. I said darn I always wished for that.

I was in the doctors office one day when the nurse said, "lets measure you". I said fine, she said "you're five feet one inches". I said "no I'm five feet three inches". To which she said "not any more!" I thought, I shrunk, I was shocked!

Guess what my Mother told me one day. She said, "When my Sandi was about six her father said he didn't like her. Liked Dawna better." She ran into closet and cried. I said, "Mother you never told me." Some father he was!

I have these comments on marriage.

My husband was not mentally 100% with me with my first marriage. Because of girlfriend he met before me, a bad situation!

A guy said to me recently he thought this way.

Marriage should be one year wait getting in to it and a three day exit getting out of it.

Diving into marriage quickly is not always the best idea in the world.

Similar interests do help. But opposites do attract, but can cause resentment in time. Differences in handling money cause trouble. Discuss who is better at it.

I thought my husbands were insane in how they handled money. It wasn't my way. The anger was there!

Don't make mistake I made – didn't take enough pictures! Of me and kids.

20) Assisted Living

Health problems

Stomach

Nose surgery

Hernia

Shingles

Foot surgery

Cysts

This one came down funny. I went to a natural doctor to see about a stomach problem, he sent me to an allergist to see about a possible food allergy. Tests came back negative ok. Allergist sent me to do a cat scan. My nose was swollen inside. He suggested surgery. – My sinuses were found to be blocked also, so they fixed that too. Talk about one thing leading to another! It took a month to recover.

The surgery caused a tear duct blockage. The eye doctor had to fix

August 3 and two weeks previous couldn't swallow meat! I did upper GI test and they found diaphragmatic hernia. Major and my stomach in surgery was upside down. Had to hold in place with tube for thirty days, four days in ICU and nine days in hospital.

One in 5,000 have it, soft diet thirty days.

Hernia caused by birth defect.

Why me?

Had walker for a while, balance off.

Later on had lupus, takes four years to get and caused by drugs.

Run down so got a virus called shingles. Back to doctor again.

My doctor said to his assistant, if I get through all of my notes in one visit, I'm doing good.

One day I yelled about bruises from blood tests. To the next one coming in he said, "good luck!" and she was perfect.

The next doctor I went to was for foot surgery, hammer toe and bunion.

My neighbor, Larry, pushed me in wheel chair to dining room for two weeks.

Hammer toe still funny, may have to do it again. This time have to break foot bone behind hammer toe and shorten it, to push toe into place. It's dislocated.

I had put some things in storage. Had help getting things out and found lock broken and a few things missing. Why me?

I've had too many people telling me what to do. I may pull out after book is finished.

I put small sticky freezer labels on new sewing machine to mark levers and save confusion.

From assisted living I rode around on Dial-a-Ride van and on the Fort Collins bus to get around town.

The bus pass was $25 per year to ride all over town.

I had my own room which was nice.

I don't remember when they decided to put me on Mellaril medication for "impulse control disorder" because of cysts in my head. I shouldn't need nursing home, just for that, right?

(2007) They suddenly put me in Mountain Crest Psych Hospital.

I called my mother too many times and she complained. I really

wasn't crazy!

I told the doctor I didn't want drugs – because I had just cured

"lupus" without drugs – in five weeks. I used things from a book

called "Nutritional Healing" from Vitamin Cottage store here.

The Mountain Crest doctor took me to court and put me on

court ordered drugs for two years. Wow!

The drugs given me were depacote, zyprexa, geoden and lithium.

The drugs caused tremors, weight gain, shaky writing, hair falling out, memory loss, head problems.

Due to not answering questions right – my doctor – basic one, sent me to a neurologist, who said: I had two types of Parkinsons' tremors from geoden and lithium. A N. P. at Mental Health said, "don't call me on lithium" -- wrong! -- I decided she didn't care much. I went back to my basic general doctor when drugs bothered me.

(2009) About June I told my Mental Health doctor I'd had enou and showed him the list of side effects of lithium from nurses book

I read. I told them to stop or I leave town and they will

never find me. It took them five months because of court

order to stop and taper off the drugs. Wow!

The doctor caught me on another day and asked me, "will

you come in and sign a paper saying you will come back and

see us again?" I said, "I will not!" and walked past his doorway!

2010

In January of 2010 I found a new neuropsychologist, Deana.

I was told I need testing, doctor OK and guardian OK to move

out.

My insurance paid $2000 for tests. I passed with average, average superior and superior.

That wasn't enough!

I've lived in assisted living for four years.

I need to drop the guardianship control to keep my sanity at this point.

I told them I wanted to leave.

I had a yard sale. I stopped when they told me to, but that wasn't enough. They called the police and an ambulance and sent me to the hospital – PVH – then Thornton Psych Hospital for forty days – real cute! – "Haven Senior Care" – near Denver.

They tried to drug me six times there. They said I knocked on car windows while crossing the street (I did not). That would have made me a danger to myself or others. The cop gave me his business card – he thought it was a strange case.

They said I could return to Spring Creek and they would give me more drugs. I said, "no!"

They sent me home and the help kept bugging me, so I walked out over night.

I walked to the bus stop and went to Loveland on errand for my mother. An antique dealer had ripped her off of some money he owed her and I went to the police station to help her out of the situation. Then I went back to bus stop and back to Fort Collins and home.

They didn't ask where I'd been just picked me up and put me in Mountain Crest Psych Hospital for two weeks. Dr Nagel, psychiatrist, was OK. He told me to get a new guardian that was a friend or relative, wait a few months and then bail out of my situation. Control freaks I don't need.

They sent me from Mountain Crest to Windsor Health Care Nursing Home which is total control. I stayed one year. I went to court with my guardian, Matthew, but he wasn't on my side.

My roommate at Windsor was a girl from a hit and run car accident. Head, hip and leg damage, walked with a cane and lift in shoe.

After one year in Windsor I petitioned the court to drop guardian. They said attorney, court visitor, more testing. June – 2011. Then move to assisted living at Oakridge, Fort

Collins about Sept. 2011.

Did occupational therapy. Then guardian said he won't release
me, March 2012.

I met a nice Catholic Chaplin who has been a big help to me in
transportation etc, etc, and things I've needed, his name is "Skip"
Tillman. We met at Windsor where his church is – he lives in For
Collins. He's a good friend.

Skip has been a guardian for some of the people at Windsor Health Care. So I asked him if he could be my guardian as my friend. His lawyer said if there are no objections it should be fine. This may turn my life around.

I keep wondering if maybe the doctors, etc. just wanted to keep my insurance money in the system so they could run all the tests on me.

I've had enough up to now!

It's now 2015.

Dr. Nagel said

I was

the "Poster Child"

Of

mental health.

I hope you

liked

my book.

Printed in the United States
By Bookmasters